Annihilationism
and
Eternal Punishment

A Biblical Examination of the Debate
Over the Destiny of the Unsaved

F. Wayne Mac Leod

Annihilationism and Eternal Punishment

Copyright © 2018 by F. Wayne Mac Leod

Table of Contents

Preface

There is a growing debate in Christian circles over what the Bible teaches about the eternal destiny of the unsaved. Of course, the traditional Christian view has been that those who do not know the Lord Jesus as their personal Saviour are destined for hell and eternal punishment. The idea is that they live forever in conscious awareness of their torment.

Annihilationism, however, states that while there will be a punishment for sinners, that punishment will not last forever. Robert Peterson defines annihilationism as follows:

> *Annihilationism is the view that lost people in hell will be exterminated after they have paid the penalty for their sin. (Robert Peterson, "Annihilationism or Eternal Punishment? Retrieved from https://www.ligonier.org/learn/articles/annihilation-or-eternal-punishment/)*

Probably the most famous contemporary evangelical theologian to call for greater acceptance of the doctrine of annihilation was John Stott. This brought him into conflict with those who held a more traditional view. Stott is quoted as saying:

> *Emotionally, I find the concept [of eternal conscious torment] intolerable and do not understand how people can live with it*

without either cauterizing their feelings or cracking under the strain. (John Stott Annihilationism, Retrieved from https://allaboutgod.com/john-stott-annihilationism-faq.htm)

His emotional struggle with the doctrine of eternal punishment is understandable. Whether we believe in the eternal punishment of the lost or not, there should be in our hearts a deep sense of grief over the thought of an unending terror and separation from the God of all comfort.

In their booklet "Heaven & Hell, What Does the Bible Really Teach?" the United Church of God states:

"Would a merciful and loving God inflict excruciating torment on human beings for trillions upon trillions of years—throughout all eternity without end? Could the Creator God of the universe be so unfeeling and uncaring? (pg. 4)

How do you comfort the parents of an unsaved teen who lies in the coffin at the gravesite? It is not easy to reflect on his or her future, apart from God. Human nature, as evil as it is, wants to offer hope to those parents.

The debate between annihilation and eternal is not limited to emotions and personal understanding of the character of God. People from both sides seek to back up their positions from Scripture. The discussion also centres around an understanding of Biblical texts and theology.

As easy as it would be to avoid this study, the questions being debated are serious. What is the character of God? What is the nature of sin? From what did Christ come to save us? Does humanity have an immortal soul? What is death, and is it the complete cessation of all consciousness? What do we do when we don't understand God and His ways? What do we do when we don't like what Scripture teaches? These questions are of fundamental importance for us in the Christian life.

I trust that this study will bring some clarity to this debate. May God be pleased also to use it to bring greater harmony in His body and greater glory to Him as the Triune God.

F. Wayne Mac Leod

Chapter 1 -
The Character of God

I am going to begin with the understanding that the reader has a basic knowledge of the teaching of Scripture about the punishment of the wicked and the doctrine of heaven and hell. Inevitably, in any discussion about eternal punishment, the conversation turns to our understanding of God's character. An article published by the United Church of God captures this well when it says:

Many who profess Christianity believe the wicked will burn forever in hell. They sincerely believe this is what the Bible teaches. But we need to ask a simple question: Would a merciful and loving God inflict excruciating torment on human beings for trillions upon trillions of years—throughout all eternity without end? Could the Creator God of the universe be so unfeeling and uncaring? (Heaven and Hell, What Does the Bible Really Teach? Published by United Church of God, 2009, page 4)

Those who oppose the idea of eternal conscious suffering in hell point us to the love and mercy of God. For them, it is inconceivable that a God of love and compassion would allow anyone to suffer forever. If even in our sinful hearts we are capable of feeling empathy for the worst criminal, how much more would a perfect God grieve for those who suffer terrible pain and agony, no matter how sinful they were. Did the Lord not love and show mercy toward us when we were sinners? Doesn't His grace extend even to those who have turned against Him? He showed compassion and offered forgiveness to the apostle Paul when he was dragging Christians out of their homes and persecuting them for believing in Jesus the Messiah (Acts 9:1-5). Does the doctrine of the eternal conscious punishment of the wicked undermine the mercy and love of God?

It is not just the mercy and love of God that is brought into question but also the justice of God. Again, let me quote from the article "Heaven and Hell, What Does the Bible Really Teach?"

The Bible indeed says that God "has appointed a day on which He will judge the world in righteousness"(Acts 17:31). At that time, those who have repented and accepted Jesus Christ as their Savior will be given eternal life. "Salvation is found in no one else, for there is no other name under heaven given to men by which we may be saved" (Acts 4:12, New International Version). But what will happen in that day to the hapless people who have never even heard or been exposed to that name? Will they be cast shrieking into hellfire alone with those who knowingly hate and despise God?

Only a minority of the earth's population lays claim to being Christian. Those who profess Christianity total only about a third of the world's population. Vast numbers of the other two-thirds have never had the opportunity to genuinely repent and accept Christ simply because of where they live. Millions more through the centuries likewise never had the opportunity because of when they lived. Would it be just and right for God to subject them to the same punishment He will give to those who willingly reject Him and choose to make themselves His enemies? (Heaven and

Annihilation and Eternal Punishment

Hell, What Does the Bible Really Teach? Published by United Church of God, 2009, page 5)

Does the doctrine of eternal conscious punishment in hell call the justice of God into question? Is there an imbalance in the judgment of God if He punishes the sinner forever for something they did or did not do in a mere seventy or eighty years of life on earth? Would it not be more just for God to destroy the body and soul of those who have sinned against him? Would not justice be served by annihilating the sinner rather than keeping them alive forever in terror and agony?

Consider also the holiness of God. As a holy God, our Creator cannot tolerate sin and rebellion. How do we reconcile the holiness of God with the fact that He allows sinners and rebellion against Him to remain for all eternity in hell? Does an eternal hell give Satan victory? Is this not what Satan has been longing for – perpetual rebellion against God? Is hell a kingdom set up in opposition to God? Will hell not prove that Satan got his way, and Christ did not ultimately defeat him? Would a holy God allow sin and rebellion to continue in hell for all eternity? Would a righteous God not choose to destroy sin and all hint of resistance, proving His total victory over it rather than to isolate it and allow it to continue?

For many people, it is impossible to reconcile what they know about God with the idea of eternal conscious punishment of the wicked in hell. The annihilation of both the body and soul in hell is easier to accept.

The Character of God

As compelling as these arguments are, we dare not reduce God to human understanding. Some time ago now I was in a local print shop. I was picking up a book I had written. A young man came in and saw what I was picking up and started a conversation with me. Seeing that the book was religious, he shared with me that he had problems with the Christian doctrine of the Trinity. He told me that it made no sense to him and, therefore, he could not accept it as true.

I still remember the words the Lord gave me that day. In response to his statement, I said: "I am glad there are things about God I cannot understand. If I could understand everything about God, He would be no bigger than my brain. I need a God that is bigger than me and what I can understand."

I am mentioning this incident because the Lord gave me those words, not just for that young man but also for myself. I often go back to that conversation and listen again to those words. I cannot pretend to understand all there is about God. He is bigger than my capacity to understand Him. He defies my human logic and reason. We often believe that that we can put God in a box. We feel that we know all there is about God and His character.

I have been married to my wife for over thirty-eight years now, but there are things about me she does not understand and things about her that I do not understand. We share a common human nature, but I cannot say that I know her perfectly. How small is a god we can know better than our friends and loved ones? There will always be a mystery to God. We will have to accept certain things by faith even when we cannot possibly understand them?

Annihilation and Eternal Punishment

Those who say that a God of mercy would never permit a person to suffer throughout all eternity will also struggle to understand why there is so much suffering in this world today. Why does a merciful God allow diseases to ravage the earth stripping parents from their children? Why does a God of justice enable a government to exist that brings hardship to Christians around the world? Why does a God of holiness allow abuse and crime to ravage this earth as we know it today? Why do floods, storms and other natural catastrophes cause the death of many people every year? History is filled with violence, oppression, injustice and abuse. Where is God in all of this?

We have all met people who refuse to believe in the God of the Bible because they cannot reconcile what is happening in the world or their personal history with what the Bible says about Him. "I cannot believe in a God who would allow this or that to happen," they say.

After completing Bible school, I went to university to do a degree in Religious Studies. One of the things I quickly discovered at university was that faith was considered a weakness. To the keen minds of these religious studies professors, everything needed to be scientific, logical and understandable to the human spirit. Human logic and reason were elevated to the point where they became the judge of what was true or false. There was no room for accepting what could not be proven intellectually or scientifically.

For the believer, however, human logic and reason are not the judges of truth and error. The Word of God, as contained in the pages of Scripture, must be our guide. The Bible reveals the character of God and His purpose. There are times when we do not understand why God has determined that we do things in a certain way, but we accept this as being from Him and submit. There is a tendency in our day to elevate human reason over the Bible. There is little room in the church for blind acceptance of the truth. We need to understand it, or we can't accept it.

This need to understand why we do things the way we do or believe what we believe has had some positive benefits for the church, but it has also been the source of many problems. In our attempt to understand everything, we also question everything. We elevate our understanding above God and His purpose. If we don't agree with what the Bible seems to be saying, we have a hard time accepting it and will do everything we can to explain away the clear command of God.

Will we reject a God we cannot understand? Will we replace Him with a theological idol that is more appealing to us? Or will we accept that there are things about God we will never grasp? Will we see faith as the weakness of those who cannot understand? Or will we accept the mysterious ways of God and trust Him when those ways make absolutely no sense to our human mind?

The challenge for us in this study is to see what the Word of God teaches and to accept it even if we cannot reconcile all the details in our human way of thinking. I dare say that we will never come to a complete understanding of God and His ways in this life. There will be much about Him we will not comprehend. Those who reject what they cannot understand, however, miss out on some of the greatest blessings God has to offer.

Chapter 2 -
A God of Justice and Wrath

In all our talk about the love, mercy and compassion of God, we sometimes forget that the Lord does become angry. As a God of justice, He demands payment for sin. A few years ago, I was speaking with a neighbour. He told me that he could not accept a God who would sentence people to hell.

I answered him by saying: "Isn't it interesting that when it comes to criminals in our society, we demand justice. If a murderer or child molester has his or her sentence reduced and is released early from prison, we are angry with the judicial system. When it comes to God, however, we expect that He will ignore our sin out of compassion and love. Should we expect less of God than our worldly law enforcement officers?"

God placed Adam and Eve in the Garden of Eden to care for it and enjoy its blessings. The one command of God was that they refrain from eating of the Tree of the Knowledge of Good and Evil. He would punish anyone who ate from that tree:

[2] And the woman said to the serpent, "We may eat of the fruit of the trees in the garden, [3] but God said, 'You shall not eat of the fruit of the tree that is in the midst of the garden, neither shall you touch it, lest you die.'" (Genesis 3)

Notice that the punishment for eating from the forbidden tree was death. When Eve ate from that tree and gave its fruit to Adam, she and her husband experienced the reality of that death. For the first time, they knew shame and hid their naked bodies from each other (Genesis 3:7). Brokenness came to their marriage. When God came into the garden to speak with them, Adam and Eve hid out of fear (Exodus 3:8-10). They experienced separation from God.

As a result of this disobedience, God told Eve that she would experience pain in childbearing. Adam would eat the fruit of the earth through the pain of hard toil (3:16-17). Pain and suffering were introduced into the world. The land would be cursed and produce its fruit only with reluctance (Genesis 3:17-18).

Finally, the Lord told Adam and Eve that they would ultimately return to dust. The bodies God had given them would age with time and one day cease to exist. Physical death was the result of this disobedience.

Let's bring this up to our present day. Ever since the sin of Adam and Eve in the garden, humanity has suffered brokenness in relationships with each other and with God. Every abuse and criminal act committed against another human being has its roots in the soil of Eden. Every war with its death and destruction is the result of the sin that entered this world. Pain, suffering and disease all trace their origin to that first rebellious act. The sickness of the earth as a result of the curse of sin has resulted in natural catastrophes and the loss of countless lives. Every life laid down in death is evidence of what took place in the Garden of Eden.

I have often heard people blaming God for all this evil. It is not God who is to blame, but sin and its curse. It was Adam and Eve who chose to disobey and open the door to sin. The fault lies squarely on their shoulders. While God did not bring sin to this earth, the question we need to examine in this context is this: Why does He allow us to suffer under its consequences?

Some people tell us that a loving and merciful God would remove all these consequences from us so that we did not have to experience tragedy and suffering in life. These people question why God would even put a forbidden tree in the Garden.

While the answers to these questions merit another book, suffice it to say that true love and devotion require a choice. God gave Adam and Eve the opportunity to love and obey Him from the heart —they chose disobedience. Their love was not forced. Nor was it a love offered because there was no other option —before them was the option to walk away from fellowship. That is what they chose.

God has provided the solution for the problem of sin—His very own Son. The Lord Jesus paid the penalty for the sin of the world. He now offers us an alternative to the curse of sin and death. Those who come to Him can experience this victory. To refuse the solution is to remain under the curse of sin and death. The penalty for sin demanded the slaughtering of God's Son. God would not bypass justice.

The sin that ravaged the earth deeply grieved the heart of God. As it increased, we read in Genesis 6:

> *[5] The LORD saw that the wickedness of man was great in the earth, and that every intention of the thoughts of his heart was only evil continually. [6] And the LORD regretted that he had made man on the earth, and it grieved him to his heart. [7] So the LORD said, "I will blot out man whom I have created from the face*

of the land, man and animals and creeping things and birds of the heavens, for I am sorry that I have made them." (Genesis 6)

Notice how God's heart grieved because of the evil in the human spirit. Note the response of God to sin in the days of Noah. God determined that He would destroy every man, woman, animal, bug and bird He created. In the days that followed, the great flood did just that. Apart from Noah, his family and the animals in the ark, the waters destroyed all living creatures.

In the days of Moses, the people of Israel turned against God when Aaron set up a golden calf in their midst. Listen to the response of God to this incident in Deuteronomy 9:

[13] "Furthermore, the LORD said to me, 'I have seen this people, and behold, it is a stubborn people. [14] Let me alone, that I may destroy them and blot out their name from under heaven. And I will make of you a nation mightier and greater than they.'
(Deuteronomy 9)

It was in the mind of God to destroy the entire nation of Israel and raise other people to be His own. This may very well have happened, were it not for the intercession of Moses on their behalf.

In Numbers 16, Korah and his sons led a revolt against Moses. They resented the fact that he was the leader and that God spoke only to him. God told Moses to separate the people from Korah and his family. The Lord then opened the earth, and the entire family of Korah and their worldly possessions were swallowed up.

When the people of Israel complained about the death of Korah's descendants, the Lord responded:

Annihilation and Eternal Punishment

[43] And Moses and Aaron came to the front of the tent of meeting, [44] and the LORD spoke to Moses, saying, [45] "Get away from the midst of this congregation, that I may consume them in a moment." And they fell on their faces. (Numbers 16)

A great plague fell on the nation of Israel for questioning the justice of God. Fourteen thousand seven hundred people died that day (not counting the family of Korah). Numbers 16 leaves us to believe that more people would have died were it not for the intervention of Moses and Aaron pleading for their lives.

As the people of God prepared to cross over the Jordan River into the Promised Land, Moses warned them about turning from God to serve idols:

[23] Take care, lest you forget the covenant of the LORD your God, which he made with you, and make a carved image, the form of anything that the LORD your God has forbidden you. [24] For the LORD your God is a consuming fire, a jealous God. [25] "When you father children and children's children, and have grown old in the land, if you act corruptly by making a carved image in the form of anything, and by doing what is evil in the sight of the LORD your God, so as to provoke him to anger, [26] I call heaven and earth to witness against you today, that you will soon utterly perish from the land that you are going over the Jordan to possess. You will not live long in it, but will be utterly destroyed. (Deuteronomy 4)

Moses describes the God of Israel as a jealous God of consuming fire (verse 24). He warned his people about making idols and told them that if they did so, they would "perish from the land" and be "utterly destroyed" (verse 26).

Moses would go on to tell Israel what would happen if after entering the Promise Land they intermarried with the ungodly foreigners of the land:

[3] You shall not intermarry with them, giving your daughters to their sons or taking their daughters for your sons, [4] for they would turn away your sons from following me, to serve other gods. Then the anger of the LORD would be kindled against you, and he would destroy you quickly. (Deuteronomy 7)

If they intermarried with the foreigners of Canaan, the anger of the Lord would be kindled against them, and H would destroy them quickly. To prevent this from happening, notice what Israel was to do:

[2] and when the LORD your God gives them over to you, and you defeat them, then you must devote them to complete destruction. You shall make no covenant with them and show no mercy to them. (Deuteronomy 7)

Israel was to kill every inhabitant of the land. They were to show no mercy.

This is not the only time the Lord issued such a command. In 1 Samuel 15, Samuel the prophet came to King Saul with these words:

[15:1] And Samuel said to Saul, "The LORD sent me to anoint you king over his people Israel; now therefore listen to the words of the LORD. [2] Thus says the LORD of hosts, 'I have noted what Amalek did to Israel in opposing them on the way when they came up out of Egypt. [3] Now go and strike Amalek and devote to destruction all that they have. Do not spare them, but kill both

*man and woman, child and infant, ox and sheep, camel and
donkey.'" (1 Samuel 15)*

God commanded Saul to wage war against the Amalekites. In this
battle, Saul was not to show any compassion. He was to destroy
the people, killing both men and women. He was to slaughter the
young children as well as infants in arms. No animal was to be
spared. No living creature was to be left alive. It was the will of God
to protect His people from the sins of the nations.

Sometimes we believe that God is obligated to show mercy to His
people. The Bible teaches, however, that God is under no such
obligation. Justice demands punishment. Will we condemn our
earthly judges because they do not show mercy toward a hardened
criminal? Are they in error if they chose to make them pay for their
illegal acts?

Listen to the words of God through His prophet Hosea.

*[6] She conceived again and bore a daughter. And the LORD said
to him, "Call her name No Mercy, for I will no more have mercy on
the house of Israel, to forgive them at all. (Hosea 1)*

God spoke clearly to His people through the birth of Hosea's child,
telling them that He would no longer have mercy on them or
forgive them.

Speaking to Jeremiah, the prophet, the Lord commanded:

*[14] "Therefore do not pray for this people, or lift up a cry or
prayer on their behalf, for I will not listen when they call to me in
the time of their trouble. (Jeremiah 11)*

Jeremiah was not to pray for his people or bring their needs to God. God told him that He would not listen to any prayer for them. While they would call out to Him in their trouble, God would not listen. God is not obligated to listen to our prayers for help. He is not a servant that we can command to do whatever we want.

When Jesus arrived at the temple of Jerusalem during the Passover and saw the money changers and merchants, He was greatly angered. That day He found some cords and made a whip out of them. With whip in hand, He forcibly drove the animals, merchants and money changers out. He overturned their tables in explosive rage over the desecration of the temple of His Father (see John 2:13-17).

When Ananias and his wife came to present their offering to God and lied about how much he made from the sale of their property, Peter openly condemned them for lying to the Holy Spirit. That day God struck them both dead for their sin. He would show no compassion on them for their lies (see Acts 5).

The apostle Peter reminds us that a Day of Judgement is coming for the earth:

[10] But the day of the Lord will come like a thief, and then the heavens will pass away with a roar, and the heavenly bodies will be burned up and dissolved, and the earth and the works that are done on it will be exposed. [11] Since all these things are thus to be dissolved, what sort of people ought you to be in lives of holiness and godliness, [12] waiting for and hastening the coming of the day of God, because of which the heavens will be set on fire and dissolved, and the heavenly bodies will melt as they burn! (2 Peter 3)

Annihilation and Eternal Punishment

The wrath of God will be poured out on this earth in the end times. Peter tells us that the heavens, as we know them, will be set on fire and dissolved.

As pleasant as the mercy and compassion of God are, we need to understand that God is also a God of justice and wrath. He is not obligated to show kindness toward us. He is not unjust for punishing sin.

No child likes the anger of a father or mother. But whether we like it or not, this is who God is. He does not sin by giving us what we deserve. Any kindness shown toward us is a gracious choice, not an obligation. God can intervene in our lives or leave us to our own devices and outcomes. He is right in being angry with sin. He is just in punishing it.

One thing is sure; we cannot change God. Scripture portrays Him as a God of compassion and kindness but also as a God of justice and wrath. We have one of two choices to make when it comes to God. We can accept Him as He is, or we can turn from Him and make our own theological idol comprised of all the elements we like and throw out the characteristics that don't appeal to us. If you do this, however, be aware of the prophetic words of Moses to Israel:

[25] "When you father children and children's children, and have grown old in the land, if you act corruptly by making a carved image in the form of anything, and by doing what is evil in the sight of the LORD your God, so as to provoke him to anger, [26] I call heaven and earth to witness against you today, that you will soon utterly perish from the land that you are going over the Jordan to possess.

You will not live long in it, but will be utterly destroyed. (Deuteronomy 4)

The question is often asked, "How could a God of love and mercy send a person to hell?" The question supposes that God is only a God of mercy and love. It does not take the whole character of God into consideration. To say that God is only loving or only merciful is to present a God that is not found in the Bible. We must accept God as He is, not for who we want Him to be.

Chapter 3 - The Reality of Hell

In the last chapter, we examined the teaching of Scripture about the justice and anger of God. It now falls on us to see what the New Testament has to say about hell as a place of punishment and suffering. This is not a comfortable topic. It would be so much easier for us to believe that those who receive the Lord Jesus receive eternal life and those who reject Him perish in the grave. This is not the teaching of the Bible, however.

Resurrection and Judgement

Speaking to Governor Felix in Acts 24, the apostle Paul said:

[15] having a hope in God, which these men themselves accept, that there will be a resurrection of both the just and the unjust. (Acts 24)

The apostle makes it quite clear in this verse that there will be a resurrection of both the "just and the unjust." Death is not the end for us, whether we accept the Lord Jesus or not. Both believers and unbelievers alike will be raised from the dead.

This was the teaching of the Lord Jesus in John 5:28-19:

[28] Do not marvel at this, for an hour is coming when all who are in the tombs will hear his voice [29] and come out, those who have done good to the resurrection of life, and those who have done evil to the resurrection of judgment. (John 5)

Jesus taught his disciples that there is a day coming when both the righteous and the unrighteous will hear His voice and rise from the dead. According to Jesus, there will be a resurrection of life and a resurrection of judgment. Both the believer and the unbeliever will be raised from the dead.

The apostle John describes this in his vision in Revelation 20 when he says:

[12] And I saw the dead, great and small, standing before the throne, and books were opened. Then another book was opened, which is the book of life. And the dead were judged by what was written in the books, according to what they had done. [13] And the sea gave up the dead who were in it, Death and Hades gave up the dead who were in them, and they were judged, each one of them, according to what they had done. [14] Then Death and Hades were thrown into the lake of fire. This is the second death, the lake of fire. [15] And if anyone's name was not found written in the book of life, he was thrown into the lake of fire. (Revelation 20)

There can be no doubt for those who examine the Scripture that there is a judgement after death. This judgement takes place after the resurrection of the body from the grave. This seems to be saying that we will face the Lord in the flesh and not just in spirit. Our death on this earth is not the end. Unbelievers will be resurrected from the dead to stand before their Creator in the flesh. At that time, they will receive their sentences.

Annihilation and Eternal Punishment

The Nature of the Judgement to Come

Understanding that we will all stand before God after the resurrection, the next matter we need to address is this: What is the sentence for those who have rejected the Lord Jesus and His offer of eternal life? A variety of New Testament passages hint at the nature of this judgement.

Listen to the words of Jesus in Mark 9:

[43] And if your hand causes you to sin, cut it off. It is better for you to enter life crippled than with two hands to go to hell, to the unquenchable fire. [45] And if your foot causes you to sin, cut it off. It is better for you to enter life lame than with two feet to be thrown into hell. [47] And if your eye causes you to sin, tear it out. It is better for you to enter the kingdom of God with one eye than with two eyes to be thrown into hell, [48] 'where their worm does not die and the fire is not quenched.' (Mark 9)

Here in this passage, the Lord Jesus told His listeners that it would be better for them to cut off their hand or foot and go through life crippled than to face the judgement to come. It was preferable to pluck out their eye than to be thrown into hell. In other words, the worst suffering that could be inflicted on the body on earth was nothing compared to the agony of hell.

One day Jesus was met by a Gentile centurion who asked Him to heal his servant. This centurion did not feel worthy of having the Lord come to his home, so he asked Him simply to speak the word, and his servant would be healed. In response to this example of faith, Jesus said:

[10] When Jesus heard this, he marveled and said to those who followed him, "Truly, I tell you, with no one in Israel have I found such faith. [11] I tell you, many will come from east and west and recline at table with Abraham, Isaac, and Jacob in the kingdom of heaven, [12] while the sons of the kingdom will be thrown into the outer darkness. In that place there will be weeping and gnashing of teeth." (Matthew 8)

Jesus declared that men and women like this Gentile would be with Him in heaven while many of the Jewish faith would be thrown into outer darkness where there would be "weeping and gnashing of teeth." The expression "weeping and gnashing of teeth" is an important one as it shows us the nature of the punishment to come. The Greek word for weeping is "dakryo," which refers to quiet grief with tears. The second word, "gnashing," however, comes from the root "klaio," which describes a loud cry of pain and agony.

Revelation 20:10 has this to say about the lake of fire (hell):

[10] and the devil who had deceived them was thrown into the lake of fire and unbelievers where the beast and the false prophet were, and they will be tormented day and night forever and ever. (Revelation 20)

What is crucial for us to note here is the word "tormented." The devil, the beast and the false prophet who were thrown into this lake of fire, were exposed to torment.

The Bible describes hell as a "hell of fire" (Matthew 5:22), "eternal fire" (Matthew 25:41), "a lake of fire and sulphur" (Revelation 20:10). It is also portrayed as a place of "gloomy darkness" (2 Peter

2:4), and a bottomless pit filled with smoke and darkness (Revelation 9:1). According to the New Testament, hell is a place of suffering, torment, weeping and intense suffering.

Those who Receive the Judgement of Hell

The Bible teaches that there will be a resurrection of the just and the unjust. It also confirms the reality of punishment in hell and that it is a place of suffering and torment. The final question we want to address here is this: Who will be sentenced to hell?

The apostle Paul answers this question when he wrote to the Thessalonians.

[8] in flaming fire, inflicting vengeance on those who do not know God and on those who do not obey the gospel of our Lord Jesus. [9] They will suffer the punishment of eternal destruction, away from the presence of the Lord and from the glory of his might, (2 Thessalonians 1)

Paul speaks of two groups of people in this passage. He tells us that God will inflict vengeance on those who do not know Him, and on those who do not obey the gospel. These individuals, says the apostle, will "suffer the punishment of eternal destruction, away from the presence of the Lord and the from glory of His might."

Hebrews 10:26-27 adds another group to this list:

[26] For if we go on sinning deliberately after receiving the knowledge of the truth, there no longer remains a sacrifice for sins, [27] but a fearful expectation of judgment, and a fury of fire that will consume the adversaries. [28] Anyone who has set aside

the law of Moses dies without mercy on the evidence of two or three witnesses. [29] How much worse punishment, do you think, will be deserved by the one who has trampled underfoot the Son of God, and has profaned the blood of the covenant by which he was sanctified, and has outraged the Spirit of grace? (Hebrews 10)

The writer to the Hebrews speaks in these verses about those who deliberately continue in sin even though they have heard the truth and understood it. These individuals should expect a "judgement and a fury of fire that will consume" (verse 27).

In Revelation 21:8, the apostle John shares the words give to him by the one who was seated on the throne of heaven:

[8] But as for the cowardly, the faithless, the detestable, as for murderers, the sexually immoral, sorcerers, idolaters, and all liars, their portion will be in the lake that burns with fire and sulfur, which is the second death." (Revelation 21)

These individuals have lived their lives apart from the gospel and its influence on their lives. According to John, their destiny in the "lake that burns with fire and sulphur."

In Matthew 23, the Lord Jesus rebukes the hypocritical religious leaders and says:

[33] You serpents, you brood of vipers, how are you to escape being sentenced to hell? (Matthew 23)

Jesus would explain that these religious leaders had misled those under their authority and drove them from the kingdom of God.

Annihilation and Eternal Punishment

[15] Woe to you, scribes and Pharisees, hypocrites! For you travel across sea and land to make a single proselyte, and when he becomes a proselyte, you make him twice as much a child of hell as yourselves. (Matthew 23)

Notice how the Lord Jesus describes these religious leaders as "children of hell." They served the cause of religion, but they drove people from God. They would be sentenced to hell.

While it is not our place to go into detail about the beasts of the end times, Revelation 19 is quite clear about their destiny:

[10] and the devil who had deceived them was thrown into the lake of fire and sulfur where the beast and the false prophet were, and they will be tormented day and night forever and ever. (Revelation 19)

Notice here that the devil, the beast and the false prophet were all thrown into the lake of fire and sulphur to be tormented day and night forever.

The judgement of hell, according to the teaching of Jesus and the apostles is reserved for a long list of individuals:

1) Those who do not know God
2) Those who do not obey the gospel
3) Those who know the truth but deliberately go on sinning
4) Cowards, the faithless, detestable people, murderers, the sexually immoral, sorcerers, idolaters, liars
5) Hypocritical religious leaders
6) The Beast and his false prophet
7) Satan and his demons

The Reality of Hell

There is no question in the minds of Jesus and the apostles that hell and judgement were a reality after the resurrection of the body. We will all be raised from the dead to face our Creator. Some will enter the presence of their Saviour. Others will be separated from Him and sent to suffer in hell.

I confess that these words are hard to write but they do convey the teaching of the Bible that: *"an hour is coming when all who are in the tombs will hear his voice [29] and come out, those who have done good to the resurrection of life, and those who have done evil to the resurrection of judgment. (John 5).*

Chapter 4 - Is Hell Eternal?

We have seen that hell, as a place of suffering and torment, is a concept taught by both Jesus and the apostles. The next question we need to address relates to what the Bible teaches about the eternal nature of hell. Is hell eternal or temporary? Let me be clear here. I am not speaking about the suffering of those who are cast into hell in this chapter. My goal is to establish whether the Bible teaches that hell, as a place, is eternal.

Unquenchable Fire

Let's begin with the words of John the Baptist to the religious leaders of his day in Matthew 3:

[11] "I baptize you with water for repentance, but he who is coming after me is mightier than I, whose sandals I am not worthy to carry. He will baptize you with the Holy Spirit and fire. [12] His winnowing fork is in his hand, and he will clear his threshing floor and gather his wheat into the barn, but the chaff he will burn with unquenchable fire." (Matthew 3)

John warns the religious leaders who had come to hear him speak that the Lord Jesus, who was coming after him, would bring judgement to this earth. Comparing humanity to a threshing floor, he told them that Jesus would separate the wheat from the chaff. The wheat would be safely stored in His barn, but the chaff would be burned with unquenchable fire. John speaks here of heaven and hell and the judgement to come. He describes hell as a place of "unquenchable fire." The term seems to indicate that the fire of hell will never go out.

Jesus repeats this imagery of hell as a place of "unquenchable fire" in Mark 9 when He says:

[43] And if your hand causes you to sin, cut it off. It is better for you to enter life crippled than with two hands to go to hell, to the unquenchable fire. (Mark 9)

Both John the Baptist and Jesus speak of hell as a place of unquenchable fire. That is to say, a place where the fires continue to burn and cannot be put out.

Eternal Fire

In Matthew 25:4, Jesus has this to say to those who had rejected Him:

[41] "Then he will say to those on his left, 'Depart from me, you cursed, into the eternal fire prepared for the devil and his angels. (Matthew 25)

Notice the term "eternal fire" used by Jesus in this verse. Jude uses these same words when he says:

[7] just as Sodom and Gomorrah and the surrounding cities, which likewise indulged in sexual immorality and pursued unnatural desire, serve as an example by undergoing a punishment of eternal fire.

Annihilation and Eternal Punishment

An eternal fire is one that never goes out. From this, we can assume that the flames of hell will burn throughout all eternity. These flames will not be extinguished.

Where the Worm does not Die

In Mark 9 Jesus describes hell as a place where the "worm does not die, and the fire is not quenched:"

[47] And if your eye causes you to sin, tear it out. It is better for you to enter the kingdom of God with one eye than with two eyes to be thrown into hell, [48] 'where their worm does not die, and the fire is not quenched.' (Mark 9)

The word "worm" refers to a worm or maggot that feeds on dead bodies. This worm does not die but continues to feed on the death that surrounds it. The fire is not quenched, for it has an abundant source of fuel to consume.

Day and Night Forever and Ever

The apostle John tells us what will happen to the devil and his angels in Revelation 20:10:

[10] and the devil who had deceived them was thrown into the lake of fire and sulfur where the beast and the false prophet were, and they will be tormented day and night forever and ever. (Revelation 20)

We will touch on this verse later in another context. What is essential for us to note here is that the torment of the devil, the false prophet and the beast is described here to be "day and night forever and ever." The agony of these creatures was constant and eternal. "Forever and ever" implies that this would go on through all eternity without end.

Eternal Judgement

In Hebrews 6, the author challenges the Hebrews to move on to maturity in their Christian life and to build on the fundamental truths they had learned.

> *[6:1] Therefore let us leave the elementary doctrine of Christ and go on to maturity, not laying again a foundation of repentance from dead works and of faith toward God, [2] and of instruction about washings, the laying on of hands, the resurrection of the dead, and eternal judgment. (Hebrews 6)*

Notice that one of those truths they had learned was the doctrine of eternal judgment. This again is something we will touch on later in another context, but the phrase is important in this chapter. Hell is the place were this judgement takes place. If the judgement in hell is described as eternal, then the implication is that hell itself will be eternal.

The Word "Eternity"

The Greek word used for "eternity" in the New Testament is the word "aionios." It comes from the root word "aion," which means an age (in time). This has led some to say that we could interpret the word eternal to mean something that is to happen in a future period and not something that necessarily lasts forever. The nature of the words used to describe hell by Jesus and the apostles, however, make it abundantly clear that hell is not just something that will happen in the age to come but also something that will endure forever. Hell's fires are eternal or unquenchable –their flames will never be extinguished. The worms of hell will never die —they will feast perpetually on the death and decay of hell. The punishment in hell of Satan, the beast and the false prophet will be forever and ever, implying that there will be no end to their punishment. While it would be much easier to believe that hell is only temporary, this is not what it taught in Scripture. We can safely assume that hell is eternal in the sense that it will exist forever as a reminder of the wrath and anger of God against sin and rebellion.

Chapter 5 -
The Wages of Sin

In Genesis 3, we read the story of Eve's temptation in the Garden of Eden.

> *[3:1] Now the serpent was more crafty than any other beast of the field that the LORD God had made. He said to the woman, "Did God actually say, 'You shall not eat of any tree in the garden'?" [2] And the woman said to the serpent, "We may eat of the fruit of the trees in the garden, [3] but God said, 'You shall not eat of the fruit of the tree that is in the midst of the garden, neither shall you touch it, lest you die.'" (Genesis 3)*

What is significant in these verses are the words of God concerning the punishment for sin. God told the first couple that they would die if they ate from the Tree of the Knowledge of Good and Evil.

This command of God is found in Genesis 2:16-17:

> *[16] And the LORD God commanded the man, saying, "You may surely eat of every tree of the garden, [17] but of the tree of the knowledge of good and evil you shall not eat, for in the day that you eat of it you shall surely die." (Genesis 2)*

Notice the words of God to Adam that day: "for in the day that you eat of it you shall surely die" (verse 17). The phrase, "in the day that you eat," tells when they would die. Death would be immediate.

These words of God create a problem for us. Genesis 5:5 tells us that Adam lived 930 years before he died. If his death would be on the day he ate the fruit of the tree, why did he live until he was 930 years old? What was the nature of the death Adam experienced that day?

We are all very familiar with Romans 6:23 that says:

[23] For the wages of sin is death, but the gift of God is eternal life in Christ Jesus our Lord. (Romans 6)

The New Testament confirms what God told Adam in Genesis 2. Sin brings death. The question we want to address here relates to what the Bible teaches about death as the penalty for sin.

Let's return to Adam and Eve in the Garden of Eden. God told them that they would die on the day they ate from the Tree of the Knowledge of Good and Evil. To understand the nature of this death, we need to look at what took place in the days and weeks that followed their disobedience.

Death in Social Relationships

Listen to the words of Genesis 3:6-7:

[6] So when the woman saw that the tree was good for food, and that it was a delight to the eyes, and that the tree was to be desired to make one wise, she took of its fruit and ate, and she also gave some to her husband who was with her, and he ate. [7] Then the eyes of both were opened, and they knew that they were naked. And they sewed fig leaves together and made themselves loincloths. (Genesis 3)

Adam and Eve were together in the garden when they ate from the forbidden tree. Notice what happened as they wiped the juice of the fruit from their faces— "the eyes of both were opened, and they knew that they were naked. And they sewed fig leaves together and made themselves loincloths" (verse 7). The passage leads us to believe that the immediate result of eating the fruit was an awareness of their nakedness and shame that made them hide that nakedness from each other. A barrier came between them as a couple. They pulled back from one another in shame. They hid from each other. The innocence was gone. There was a break in personal relationships. With the entrance of sin, there was cause to be fearful. Evil thoughts and desires would now plague every relationship from that point forward. Adam and Eve would experience this personally, but more specifically, they would experience this in the relationship that existed between their sons. Their son Cain killed his brother Abel out of jealousy. From that point forward, humanity would experience this death of social relationships as sin moved them to fight and betray one another. Nation would wage war against nation. Abuse, violence against humanity, prejudice, and hatred of all kinds would ravage and devastate relationships across the globe. There was a death of social relations. That took place the moment Adam and Eve disobeyed the Lord in the garden.

Death of Relationship with God

As we move on in the story of Adam and Eve, we see something else that took place immediately. In Genesis 3:8, we read:

[8] And they heard the sound of the LORD God walking in the garden in the cool of the day, and the man and his wife hid

themselves from the presence of the LORD God among the trees of the garden. [9] But the LORD God called to the man and said to him, "Where are you?" [10] And he said, "I heard the sound of you in the garden, and I was afraid, because I was naked, and I hid myself." [11] He said, "Who told you that you were naked? Have you eaten of the tree of which I commanded you not to eat?" (Genesis 3)

It appears that the Lord God would visit with Adam and Eve in the Garden. After eating from the forbidden tree, however, the encounter between God and the couple changed. Genesis 3:8 tells us that when Adam and Eve heard the presence of God in the Garden, they hid from Him. When asked why they did so, Adam told God that he was afraid because he was naked. Adam was afraid of God and ashamed. Shame and guilt now stood between Adam and his Creator. Notice in verse 11 that God attributes this to the fact that they had eaten of the tree of the Knowledge of Good and Evil. Eating from that tree brought death in the relationship between Adam and his God. Adam now had cause for fear. He had offended a holy and just God. This death in relationship with God spread from Adam to every human being on the earth.

King David declared in Psalm 51:

[5] Behold, I was brought forth in iniquity, and in sin did my mother conceive me. (Psalm 51)

The prophet Isaiah would later declare:

[2] but your iniquities have made a separation between you and your God, and your sins have hidden his face from you so that he does not hear. (Isaiah 59)

Sin separated Adam from his God. That took place on the day that he and his wife ate from the Tree of the Knowledge of Good and Evil. That sin spread from person to person so that all were affected. Quoting from the Old Testament Psalms, the apostle Paul wrote:

[10] as it is written: "None is righteous, no, not one; (Romans 3)

From the time Adam and Eve ate from the tree in the centre of the garden onward, humankind has suffered this death in their relationship with God. We are separated from our Creator and under His judgement. Sin brought spiritual death.

Environmental Death

Listen to what God told Adam in Genesis 3:17,18:

[17] And to Adam he said, "Because you have listened to the voice of your wife and have eaten of the tree of which I commanded you, 'You shall not eat of it,' cursed is the ground because of you; in pain you shall eat of it all the days of your life; [18] thorns and thistles it shall bring forth for you; and you shall eat the plants of the field.

Creation was cursed the day Adam and Eve ate the forbidden fruit. The ground would now reluctantly yield its crops. Thorns and thistles would choke out the food produced in the soil. Adam and all humankind after him, would cultivate that fruit by sweat and hard work.

The earth as Adam knew it died that day. Sin ravages our environment. Floods, earthquakes, and other natural disasters are the result of sin. Draughts and famines are a reminder to us that the curse of sin continues to ravage our earth. Sickness and diseases brought about by environmental causes spread throughout the world. The environment, as we know it today, is in the process of death and decay.

Listen to the words of the apostle Paul in Romans 8:

[20] For the creation was subjected to futility, not willingly, but because of him who subjected it, in hope [21] that the creation itself will be set free from its bondage to corruption and obtain the freedom of the glory of the children of God. [22] For we know that the whole creation has been groaning together in the pains of childbirth until now. (Romans 8)

The apostle makes it very clear that this earth on which we live has been subject to bondage and corruption as a result of sin. It longs for the day when it will be set free to be all it was intended to be. On the day that Adam and Eve sinned, they brought the curse of death to this earth.

Physical Death

God told Adam in Genesis 3:19:

[19] By the sweat of your face you shall eat bread, till you return to the ground, for out of it you were taken; for you are dust, and to dust you shall return." (Genesis 3)

44

When we think of death, we usually think of the death of the body. God told Adam that this would also be the result of his sin. His body would age and become weaker. Eventually, his heart would stop beating, and his body would cease to function. His physical body would decay and return to dust. It should be noted that pain and suffering would also be part of this ageing and decaying of the body. God told Eve that she would give birth to children in pain (Genesis 3:16). Adam would eat of the fruit of the soil through hard work and pain (Genesis 3:17-18). From the moment Adam ate the fruit of the tree, he experienced the effect of the curse of death on his physical body. While he would not die for many years, he knew that his body was ageing, and he was living under the curse of death.

The wages of sin is death, but death is much more than what happens when we lose a loved one. Death affects relationships with people and with God. It impacts nature and the environment in which we live. Death curses every aspect of our lives. It deteriorates the quality of life. Instead of peace, it brings enmity and separation between God and His creation. Instead of health and joy, it brings sickness and sorrow. It replaces fruitfulness with barrenness. Death separates us from the fullness of God's blessing. It places us under His curse. In the hundreds of years left in Adam's life, he would live in this death and separation from God.

There is an interesting passage in Hebrews 11 that speaks about Enoch:

[5] By faith Enoch was taken up so that he should not see death, and he was not found, because God had taken him. Now before

he was taken he was commended as having pleased God.
(Hebrews 11)

We have seen that the wages of sin is death (Genesis 2:17; Romans 6:23). Here in Hebrews 11, we read, however, that Enoch did not see death. Was Enoch perfect? Could we assume from this that he never sinned and, therefore, did experience death? The verse causes a problem only if we see death to refer to the cessation of the physical functions of the body. Enoch, though he did not experience a physical death, certainly lived in a world that was under the curse of death. He experienced the effects of sin on his body and heart like every other human being. He lived separated from the fullness of God's blessings. The fact that God chose to bring him into His presence without experiencing a physical death does not diminish the fact that even Enoch lived under the curse of sin and death throughout his life.

Paul, the apostle, cried out to God in Romans 7:

[22] For I delight in the law of God, in my inner being, [23] but I see in my members another law waging war against the law of my mind and making me captive to the law of sin that dwells in my members. [24] Wretched man that I am! Who will deliver me from this body of death? (Romans 7)

The apostle saw within himself what he called a "body of death." This body of death was a part of him that waged war against the purpose of God for his life. This was his sinful nature. It hindered him in his spiritual walk, and he hated its presence in his life. He longed for deliverance from this death. The death to which the apostle refers here is not physical death but a fleshly desire that was contrary to God and His purpose. He lived daily with this death in him.

John recounts what he heard in his vision of heaven in Revelation 21:

[3] And I heard a loud voice from the throne saying, "Behold, the dwelling place of God is with man. He will dwell with them, and they will be his people, and God himself will be with them as their God. [4] He will wipe away every tear from their eyes, and death shall be no more, neither shall there be mourning, nor crying, nor pain anymore, for the former things have passed away."
(Revelation 21)

The apostle tells us that he heard a voice saying that God would wipe away every tear and death would be no more. There are several significant details we need to see here in these verses. Remember that death came as a result of sin, brought separation from God and tremendous pain and suffering on this earth. The voice that spoke in heaven that day told John that the effects of this curse would be broken. God would dwell with His people. There would no longer be any separation between them. All pain and suffering would be banished, and there would be no more cause for tears and mourning. Death would be no more. Through the work of the Lord Jesus, the curse of death would be broken. Heaven is a place where we live in absolute freedom from the effects of death in all its dimensions.

The penalty for sin is much more than the cessation of bodily and mental functions—it is a life separated from the blessings and presence of God. A quick look around us shows us just how much sin has affected us. It has cursed this earth. Not one of us is spared the pain, suffering and brokenness it brings. All of this was the result of a single act of disobedience. Every agony we have ever experienced has been the result of this sin and the curse that it brought to us. Sin must never be taken lightly. It is a deadly plague that has taken more lives than any other disease. It has ravished our earth and every single person who was ever born. It will ultimately destroy every one of us, and unless we are freed from its deadly curse, it will separate us eternally from our Creator.

What does this teaching have to do with the subject at hand? Some people say that a loving God would never allow us to suffer. He would never take a loved one from us. Those who say this need to open their eyes to the truth of Genesis 3:3. God declared the sentence of death on anyone who ate from the tree in the midst of the garden. Just take a look at the evil that surrounds you. Consider the injustice and disappointments in life. Consider the horrible atrocities of history and the abuses of our day. This is the curse of sin and death. It is the punishment of disobedience. It was the declaration of God about what would happen if Eve ate the fruit of the tree. Would a loving and compassionate God allow this to happen? If you believe in the God of Genesis, then you have to admit that He would.

Chapter 6 -
The Nature of the Soul

There is much debate over the nature of the soul. The Hebrew word used in the Old Testament is the word "nepes" which refers to the breath, thoughts and emotions. The word "nepes" is not used exclusively of human beings but applied to animals as well (Genesis 1:20; Job 41:21; Jeremiah 2:24). In the New Testament, the Greek word for soul is the word "psuche" which means to breathe or to blow. The soul is our life or breath as distinguished from our physical bodies. It is what makes us conscious of our surroundings and able to interact with our circumstances.

The soul is capable of emotions and feelings. Speaking to Jacob in Genesis 34:8 Hamor said:

[8] But Hamor spoke with them, saying, "The soul of my son Shechem longs for your daughter. Please give her to him to be his wife. (Genesis 34)

The Lord God challenged His people not to listen to false prophets for He was testing them to see if they loved Him with all their heart and soul:

[3] you shall not listen to the words of that prophet or that dreamer of dreams. For the LORD your God is testing you, to know whether you love the LORD your God with all your heart and with all your soul. (Deuteronomy 13)

The Nature of the Soul

Jesus experienced deep sorrow in His soul in Mark 14:

> *[34] And he said to them, "My soul is very sorrowful, even to death. Remain here and watch."*

The soul is the part of us that is capable of reason and emotion.

Can the Soul Die?

It is quite clear that our physical bodies will one day die. What about our souls? Can our souls die as well?

In Genesis 35, we read about the death of Rachel.

> *[18] And as her soul was departing (for she was dying), she called his name Ben-oni; but his father called him Benjamin. (Genesis 35)*

Genesis 35:18 tells us that Rachel's soul was departing and connects this with the fact that she was dying. In other words, at death, our soul leaves us. We are no longer capable of reason, feeling or experiencing life.

Listen to the words of Job in Job 33:

> *[22] His soul draws near the pit, and his life to those who bring death. (Job 33)*

Job describes the soul as drawing near the pit. The pit is the place of death—a place where life and breath are stripped away.

In Psalm 22:2, the Psalmist pleads with the Lord to deliver his soul from the sword:

> *[20] Deliver my soul from the sword, my precious life from the power of the dog! (Psalm 22)*

He takes this a step further in Psalm 33 when he says:

[18] Behold, the eye of the LORD is on those who fear him, on those who hope in his steadfast love, [19] that he may deliver their soul from death and keep them alive in famine. (Psalm 33)

Notice the reference to the fact that the Lord delivers the soul of those who fears Him from death. The Psalmist experienced deep gratitude to God for saving his soul from death in Psalm 56:

[12] I must perform my vows to you, O God; I will render thank offerings to you. [13] For you have delivered my soul from death, yes, my feet from falling, that I may walk before God in the light of life. (Psalm 56)

The Psalmist had the understanding here that the soul could die. This gratitude for saving that human soul from death is repeated often in the Psalms (see Psalm 16:10; 49:15; 86:13; 89:48; 109:31; 116:8).

The Old Testament prophets also spoke of the soul. Isaiah has this to say about the King of Assyria who boasted in his great achievements:

[18] The glory of his forest and of his fruitful land the LORD will destroy, both soul and body, and it will be as when a sick man wastes away. (Isaiah 10)

God would destroy the body and soul of his land. While not directly referring to the human soul, the concept of the death of the soul of the land is quite clear.

Speaking more directly to the human soul, Ezekiel the prophet says:

[20] The soul who sins shall die. The son shall not suffer for the iniquity of the father, nor the father suffer for the iniquity of the son. The righteousness of the righteous shall be upon himself, and the wickedness of the wicked shall be upon himself. (Ezekiel 18)

Ezekiel is quite clear here when he says that the soul of the sinner will die. The New Testament conveys the same idea. Listen to the words of Jesus in Matthew 10:

[28] And do not fear those who kill the body but cannot kill the soul. Rather fear him who can destroy both soul and body in hell. (Matthew 10)

There can be no question about what Jesus is saying here. God can destroy both the soul and the body in hell.

Jesus told a parable in Luke 12 about a rich man whose desire was to build bigger barns to store more wealth. He told His listeners that this individual was foolish because he did not take God into account. That very night God would require his soul:

[20] But God said to him, 'Fool! This night your soul is required of you, and the things you have prepared, whose will they be?' (Luke 12)

The soul of the man would be taken from him that night. He was not in control of his life.

Speaking to the people of his day, the apostle Peter said:

[23] And it shall be that every soul who does not listen to that prophet shall be destroyed from the people.' (Acts 3)

The apostle warned that the souls of those who did not listen to the words of God would be destroyed.

James tells us that if we reach out to a wandering sinner and bring him back the Lord, we will save his soul from death:

[20] let him know that whoever brings back a sinner from his wandering will save his soul from death and will cover a multitude of sins. (James 5)

While the soul dies, we need to understand that God can raise that soul to life again just as He raises the body. Consider what John describes for us in Revelation 20:

[4] Then I saw thrones, and seated on them were those to whom the authority to judge was committed. Also I saw the souls of those who had been beheaded for the testimony of Jesus and for the word of God, and those who had not worshiped the beast or its image and had not received its mark on their foreheads or their hands. They came to life and reigned with Christ for a thousand years. (Revelation 20)

Notice that the apostle saw the souls of those beheaded for Christ. These souls, he tells us, came to life and reigned with Christ for a thousand years.

There can be no doubt that the Bible teaches that the soul can die. What dies, however, will also be raised to life again at the resurrection.

Chapter 7 -
The Human Spirit

The question of whether human beings have a spirit has been debated in Christian circles. Some Christians believe that we are composed of body and soul only. Others see human beings as body, soul and spirit. When we speak of spirit in this sense, we are not speaking about the Holy Spirit, who lives in the true believer but rather a human spirit as distinct from the soul. Again, we need to return to the Scriptures to see what they have to say.

The word "spirit" as it relates to human beings occurs numerous times in the Bible. In the Old Testament, the word used is "ruah." It speaks of the Spirit of God but also of the spirit of a man or woman. For example, in Genesis 41:8, after having a troubling vision, Pharoah's spirit was troubled.

[8] So in the morning his spirit was troubled, and he sent and called for all the magicians of Egypt and all its wise men. Pharaoh told them his dreams, but there was none who could interpret them to Pharaoh. (Genesis 41)

Upon hearing that his son Joseph was alive, Jacob's spirit was revived:

[27] But when they told him all the words of Joseph, which he had said to them, and when he saw the wagons that Joseph had sent to carry him, the spirit of their father Jacob revived. (Genesis 45)

In this sense, the spirit, like the soul, can experience emotions.

The prophet Ezekiel told the people of his day that the Lord God would put a new spirit within them:

[19] And I will give them one heart, and a new spirit I will put within them. I will remove the heart of stone from their flesh and give them a heart of flesh, [20] that they may walk in my statutes and keep my rules and obey them. And they shall be my people, and I will be their God. (Ezekiel 11)

What Ezekiel was telling the people was that the Lord would change how they saw things and give them new motivation and passion in life. In this case, it would be a desire to follow God and keep His commandments. The spirit, when spoken of in this way, refers to a passion or motivation in life.

We catch a glimpse of this passion in Isaiah 26:9, where the prophet says:

[9] My soul yearns for you in the night; my spirit within me earnestly seeks you. For when your judgments are in the earth, the inhabitants of the world learn righteousness. (Isaiah 26)

Notice the connection in Isaiah 26 between the soul and the spirit. The soul yearns for God, and the spirit earnestly seeks after him. Both soul and spirit experience passion and desire.

The use of the word spirit, however, goes beyond the feeling of passion and emotions. In Exodus 28, we read:

[3] You shall speak to all the skillful, whom I have filled with a spirit of skill, that they make Aaron's garments to consecrate him for my priesthood. (Exodus 28)

The phrase "spirit of skill" shows us that the spirit in one person may be different from another. God gave certain individuals special skills to accomplish His purpose. These skills are different in each person. It was as if God breathed into these individuals these special abilities. They are divinely gifted to accomplish His purpose.

Deuteronomy 34:9 tells us that Joshua had a spirit of wisdom:

[9] And Joshua the son of Nun was full of the spirit of wisdom, for Moses had laid his hands on him. So the people of Israel obeyed him and did as the LORD had commanded Moses. (Deuteronomy 34)

What is particularly interesting in this passage is that this "spirit of wisdom" was given to him through the laying on of Moses' hands. In other words, Joshua was not born with this spirit of wisdom. It was given to him from God when Moses prayed over him.

We have already said that the spirit feels passion and desires. According to Exodus 35:21, we also see that the spirit moves and motivates people to action. The people of Moses' day were stirred in their spirit and responded accordingly. Consider the words of Exodus 35:21:

[21] And they came, everyone whose heart stirred him, and everyone whose spirit moved him, and brought the LORD's contribution to be used for the tent of meeting, and for all its service, and for the holy garments. (Exodus 35)

After falling into sin, David pleaded with God to renew His spirit:

[10] Create in me a clean heart, O God, and renew a right spirit within me. (Psalm 51)

This renewing of his spirit was something that David knew God had to do. He understood the sin of his heart and the passions of his flesh and asked God to cleanse him of this evil and put a new and right spirit in him. This new spirit would have a passion for God and His purpose.

The prophet Zechariah tells us that the Lord who created the heavens also formed the spirit of man within him:

[12:1] The oracle of the word of the LORD concerning Israel: Thus declares the LORD, who stretched out the heavens and founded the earth and formed the spirit of man within him. (Zechariah 12)

This tells us that human beings have a spirit.

Ecclesiastes 12 speaks about old age and what happens as we age. Listen to the words of verse 7:

[7] and the dust returns to the earth as it was, and the spirit returns to God who gave it. (Ecclesiastes 12)

In Genesis, the Lord told Adam and Eve that their bodies would return to the dust. Ecclesiastes 12:7 seems to refer to this when it says that the "dust returns to the earth." Notice, however, what that author has to say about the spirit –it "returns to God who gave it." It appears from this that the writer expected that while his body would die, his spirit would live on in the presence of God.

Annihilation and Eternal Punishment

As we come to the New Testament, we read the story of the crucifixion of the Lord Jesus. Matthew 27:50 tells us that when Jesus died, he "yielded up his spirit." At the death of Christ, his spirit was given up or surrendered. Luke tells us where the spirit of Jesus went:

> *[46] Then Jesus, calling out with a loud voice, said, "Father, into your hands I commit my spirit!" And having said this he breathed his last. (Luke 23)*

The spirit of Jesus was committed into the hands of the Father. Can we assume from this that the spirit of Christ could exist without His body?

It is interesting to note the words of the Stephen when he was stoned to death in Acts 7:59:

> *[59] And as they were stoning Stephen, he called out, "Lord Jesus, receive my spirit." (Acts 7)*

It appears from this that Stephen expected his body would die, and his spirit would go to the Lord Jesus. His spirit would be separated from his body and enter the presence of God.

In Luke 8, we read the story of how a man by the name of Jairus came to Jesus because his twelve-year-old daughter was sick to the point of dying. By the time Jesus arrived at their home, the funeral was already underway—Jairus' daughter had died. Jesus went over to the body, took her by the hand and commanded her to rise. Luke, the doctor, tells us what happened:

[55] And her spirit returned, and she got up at once. And he directed that something should be given her to eat. (Luke 8)

The spirit of Jairus' daughter had left her. At Jesus' command, however, that spirit returned, and she rose up from her deathbed. Again, notice the separation of the body and the spirit at her death. The returning of her spirit brought life again.

The apostle James reminds us that our life is in our spirit:

[26] For as the body apart from the spirit is dead, so also faith apart from works is dead. (James 2)

When our spirit departs, our body dies.

While there seem to be some similarities between the soul and the spirit, there are also some differences. The Bible uses different words to speak of soul and spirit in both the Old and New Testament.

The Bible seems to make it clear that the soul can die. There does not seem to be any reference in Scripture to the spirit dying. The spirit seems to depart from the body at the time of death. Jesus committed his spirit to the Father. Philip committed his to Jesus.

Scripture also seems to speak of both the soul and the spirit as being separate. Consider what Paul told the Thessalonians:

[23] Now may the God of peace himself sanctify you completely, and may your whole spirit and soul and body be kept blameless at the coming of our Lord Jesus Christ. (1 Thessalonians 5)

Paul speaks of the spirit, the soul and the body in this verse.

This is not the only place in the Bible where the soul and the spirit are mentioned as being distinct from each other.

[12] For the word of God is living and active, sharper than any two-edged sword, piercing to the division of soul and of spirit, of joints and of marrow, and discerning the thoughts and intentions of the heart. (Hebrews 4)

Notice the comparison between the joints and marrow of the bones and the thoughts and intentions of the heart. Thoughts are different from intentions, but they work together. Joints and marrow have separate functions for the bones, but they too work together. So, the soul and the spirit are independent but join forces for the purpose of God.

It is also important that we understand that the spirit we speak of here is not the Holy Spirit of God, who comes to live in the believer. Writing to the Corinthians, the apostle Paul said:

[7:1] Since we have these promises, beloved, let us cleanse ourselves from every defilement of body and spirit, bringing holiness to completion in the fear of God. (2 Corinthians 7)

Paul challenged the Corinthians to cleanse themselves from any defilement of spirit. While the human spirit can be defiled, this could not be said of the Holy Spirit, who is always free from corruption or sin in any form. The apostle would confirm this distinction between the human spirit and the Holy Spirit in Romans 8:

[16] The Spirit himself bears witness with our spirit that we are children of God (Romans 8)

Paul speaks here about "the Spirit" and "our spirit." In his mind, these were two separate entities.

Peter encouraged believers to live in the spirit. In doing so, they were following the example God had set for them:

[6] For this is why the gospel was preached even to those who are dead, that though judged in the flesh the way people are, they might live in the spirit the way God does. (1 Peter 4)

All too often, as believers, we live in the flesh. God has given us a spirit that can communicate with him, but we prefer the logic of our mind.

Paul taught the church in Corinth about the gift of tongues. Notice what he had to say to them in 1 Corinthians 14 about the gift:

[14] For if I pray in a tongue, my spirit prays but my mind is unfruitful. [15] What am I to do? I will pray with my spirit, but I will pray with my mind also; I will sing praise with my spirit, but I will sing with my mind also. [16] Otherwise, if you give thanks with your spirit, how can anyone in the position of an outsider say "Amen" to your thanksgiving when he does not know what you are saying? (1 Corinthians 14)

The gift of tongues gave the human spirit a voice. Paul taught that it was important to pray with a full understanding of the mind, but he would also pray and sing with his spirit. By praying in a tongue, Paul told the Corinthians that the mind remained unfruitful. In other words, the gift of tongues bypassed the mind. He spoke what was in his spirit but did not understand what he was saying. This did not discourage Paul. He told the Corinthians that he would pray with his spirit even if his mind did not understand. He would also ask God to give him an interpretation of what he was praying.

Paul teaches that the human spirit is distinct from the soul with its capacity to reason and understand. He prayed with his spirit while his soul was not aware of what he prayed. Notice also how he speaks of "my spirit," (verse 14, 15) and "your spirit" (verse 16). This distinguishes the human spirit from the Holy Spirit.

Let me conclude with one last verse about the human spirit. 1 Peter 3:18 has this to say about Jesus when He died on the cross:

[18] For Christ also suffered once for sins, the righteous for the unrighteous, that he might bring us to God, being put to death in the flesh but made alive in the spirit, [19] in which he went and proclaimed to the spirits in prison, [20] because they formerly did not obey, when God's patience waited in the days of Noah, while the ark was being prepared, in which a few, that is, eight persons, were brought safely through water. (1 Peter 3)

According to Peter, when the Lord Jesus died, his spirit was made alive. The spirit of Christ does not seem to be subject to death. Notice also that after He died, Jesus proclaimed to the spirits in prison. These spirits are described in verse 19 as those who "formerly did not obey." While it is not my purpose to comment on these verses here, I do want us to notice something that pertains to our study.

Peter tells us that Christ went to preach to the spirits of those who were in prison because they formerly did not obey. He connects these spirits to the time of Noah. The context indicates that these were unbelievers who rejected the Lord. They were held in a prison of some sort. The fact that the Lord Jesus proclaimed to them would lead us to believe that these spirits were consciously aware of what He proclaimed –they were not dead. We seem to have, in these verses, an example of the spirits of those who had died, living apart from their earthly body and soul.

What these verses seem to show us is that we have a human spirit. The spirit is distinct from the soul. While the Bible speaks of the soul dying, there does not seem to be any reference to the human spirit dying. Instead, it leaves the body at death and returns to God or to some other place where they await the resurrection.

Annihilationism speaks of the extermination of the human being after judgement — it basis this on the fact that the soul and the body are not eternal. Scripture does seem to indicate that the soul and the body can die. Nowhere in Scripture, however, is there any evidence that the spirit dies. It appears to live on even after the death of the body and soul in conscious awareness of its surroundings.

Chapter 8 -
What Happens at Death?

We come now to the question of what the Bible teaches about what happens after we die. I want to limit this to the period between death and judgement. The answer is not found in any one passage of Scripture, so we will have to put a variety of Bible verses together.

The Physical Body

Let's begin by examining what the Bible has to say about the human body at death. Speaking to Adam in Genesis 3, the Lord God said:

> *[19] By the sweat of your face you shall eat bread, till you return to the ground, for out of it you were taken; for you are dust, and to dust you shall return." (Genesis 3)*

The Lord God told Adam that as a result of sin, he would live his life and then die. At death, his body would return to the state it was before it was created –it would return to dust. In other words, the physical body we have right now at death will decompose in the grave.

This was the understanding of Job when he said to God:

> *[9] Remember that you have made me like clay; and will you return me to the dust? (Job 10)*

What Happens at Death?

Speaking to his friends, who came to comfort him, Job complained:

[13] If I hope for Sheol as my house, if I make my bed in darkness, [14] if I say to the pit, 'You are my father,' and to the worm, 'My mother,' or 'My sister,' [15] where then is my hope? Who will see my hope? [16] Will it go down to the bars of Sheol? Shall we descend together into the dust?" (Job 17)

Job gives us some insight into Sheol or the grave in these verses. It is a place of darkness (verse 13). It is a place where the worm dwells (verse 14). It is a place where the body returns to dust (verse 16). From this, we understand that Job believed that when his body died is was eaten by worms and ultimately returned to dust.

The psalmist fearing death proclaimed:

[15] my strength is dried up like a potsherd, and my tongue sticks to my jaws; you lay me in the dust of death. (Psalm 22)

The bodies of those who died are described in Psalm 22 as going "down to the dust:

[29] All the prosperous of the earth eat and worship; before him shall bow all who go down to the dust, even the one who could not keep himself alive. (Psalm 22)

Comparing God to human beings, the Psalmist declares:

[2] Before the mountains were brought forth, or ever you had formed the earth and the world, from everlasting to everlasting you are God. [3] You return man to dust and say, "Return, O children of man!" [4] For a thousand years in your sight are but as yesterday when it is past, or as a watch in the night. (Psalm 90)

Annihilation and Eternal Punishment

The Lord God is from everlasting to everlasting. Time does not affect God. In direct contrast to the everlasting God is man who, after a short existence, returns to dust.

Solomon compares animals and man in Ecclesiastes 3:19-20:

[19] For what happens to the children of man and what happens to the beasts is the same; as one dies, so dies the other. They all have the same breath, and man has no advantage over the beasts, for all is vanity. [20] All go to one place. All are from the dust, and to dust all return. (Ecclesiastes 3:20)

These passages make it abundantly clear that our earthly bodies will one day cease to function. They will be laid in the ground and decompose.

The Soul

We have seen that the soul also can die. Ezekiel confirmed this when he said:

[18] and say, Thus says the Lord GOD: Woe to the women who sew magic bands upon all wrists, and make veils for the heads of persons of every stature, in the hunt for souls! Will you hunt down souls belonging to my people and keep your own souls alive? [19] You have profaned me among my people for handfuls of barley and for pieces of bread, putting to death souls who should not die and keeping alive souls who should not live, by your lying to my people, who listen to lies. (Ezekiel 13)

Through Ezekiel, the Lord God accused His people of hunting down souls and putting them to death. When these souls died, it would seem reasonable to assume that they had no more conscious awareness of their surroundings.

The Psalmist tells us that the human soul is subject to the power of the grave:

[48] What man can live and never see death? Who can deliver his soul from the power of Sheol? Selah (Psalm 89)

Elihu, speaking to Job, describes the man who falls short of God's law:

[19] "Man is also rebuked with pain on his bed and with continual strife in his bones, [20] so that his life loathes bread, and his appetite the choicest food. [21] His flesh is so wasted away that it cannot be seen, and his bones that were not seen stick out. [22] His soul draws near the pit, and his life to those who bring death. (Job 33)

The man Elihu describes here is one whose "soul draws near the pit." The pit is the grave. Elihu believed that the human soul would go with the body to the grave. This is made clear when he goes on to say:

[29] "Behold, God does all these things, twice, three times, with a man, [30] to bring back his soul from the pit, that he may be lighted with the light of life. (Job 33)

Notice here that while, according to Elihu, the soul went to the grave with the body, the Lord God was also capable of raising it back to life again.

The sons of Korah spoke about the grave in Psalm 88:

[10] Do you work wonders for the dead? Do the departed rise up to praise you? Selah [11] Is your steadfast love declared in the grave, or your faithfulness in Abaddon? [12] Are your wonders known in the darkness, or your righteousness in the land of forgetfulness? (Psalm 88)

Verse 11 compares the grave to Abaddon. The word in the Hebrew language means "ruin" or "destruction." It refers to the place of the dead. The grave is also described as a place of "darkness" and a "land of forgetfulness." In this place, the love of God is not declared or felt. There does not appear to be any conscious awareness in the grave. Like the body, the soul appears to cease its function. Like the body, however, it will be raised again at the resurrection.

The Spirit

While it appears that the soul, as the consciousness of human beings and animals, ceases to function at death, this does not appear to be the case for the spirit.

1 Samuel 28 describes an incident where King Saul needed counsel. The Philistines were pressing in hard against him, and he was not sure what he was to do. He had always gone to Samuel the prophet when he needed to hear from the Lord, but Samuel had died. He tried other means to hear from the Lord, but the Lord was not answering him. In desperation, Saul determined to find a medium that could speak to the spirit of Saul.

[8] So Saul disguised himself and put on other garments and went, he and two men with him. And they came to the woman by night. And he said, "Divine for me by a spirit and bring up for me

69

whomever I shall name to you." [9] The woman said to him, "Surely you know what Saul has done, how he has cut off the mediums and the necromancers from the land. Why then are you laying a trap for my life to bring about my death?" [10] But Saul swore to her by the LORD, "As the LORD lives, no punishment shall come upon you for this thing." [11] Then the woman said, "Whom shall I bring up for you?" He said, "Bring up Samuel for me." (1 Samuel 28)

Saul asked the medium to bring up the spirit of Samuel so that he could speak with him and ask his advice. The Law of Moses forbade speaking with the spirits of the dead (see Deuteronomy 18:10,11). If the law forbade speaking to the spirits of the dead, it is safe to say that this was actually possible. This means that the spirit has some awareness and consciousness after death.

We have already seen that the Lord Jesus committed his spirit to the Father at the time of His crucifixion (Luke 23:46). When Stephen was stoned to death, committed His spirit to the Lord Jesus (see Acts 7:59). The assumption here was that the spirit would not go with them to the grave.

Writing to the Corinthians, the apostle Paul said:

[8] Yes, we are of good courage, and we would rather be away from the body and at home with the Lord. (2 Corinthians 5)

It appears that that expectation of the apostle was that when his body died, his spirit would go to be with the Lord. Paul appears to be speaking of a time after his death but before the resurrection of the body. He was absent from the body, but his spirit was in the presence of the Lord God.

Speaking to the thief on the cross beside Him, the Lord Jesus said: Truly, I say to you, today you will be with me in paradise" (Luke 23:43). The idea is that after his body died and was taken down from the cross, the spirit of this man would enter the presence of God. Notice that Jesus told him that this would be immediate—he would be with him "today."

There is very little in the Bible about the destiny of the spirit of the unbeliever before judgement. 1 Peter 3, however, may give us a clue.

[18] For Christ also suffered once for sins, the righteous for the unrighteous, that he might bring us to God, being put to death in the flesh but made alive in the spirit, [19] in which he went and proclaimed to the spirits in prison, [20] because they formerly did not obey, when God's patience waited in the days of Noah, while the ark was being prepared, in which a few, that is, eight persons, were brought safely through water. (1 Peter 3)

While this passage is not an easy one to interpret, there are several points we need to make here. Notice first that in verse 18, Peter tells us that Jesus was put to death in the flesh but made alive in the spirit. The idea seems to be that while his body was dead, His spirit was very much alive. It did not die with him on the cross.

The second point we need to notice is in verse 19, which tells us that the Lord Jesus went in spirit to proclaim to the spirits in prison who did not obey when God's patience was tested in the days of Noah. Peter does not explain what he means here. Notice, however, that the apostle speaks about a prison in which those

71

who did not obey were kept. Compare this to what the prophet Isaiah said:

> [21] On that day the LORD will punish the host of heaven, in heaven, and the kings of the earth, on the earth. [22] They will be gathered together as prisoners in a pit; they will be shut up in a prison, and after many days they will be punished. [23] Then the moon will be confounded and the sun ashamed, for the LORD of hosts reigns on Mount Zion and in Jerusalem, and his glory will be before his elders. (Isaiah 24)

Isaiah prophesied of a day when the hosts of heaven and the earth would be punished. Before that punishment, however, he said that they would be "shut up in prison, and after many days, they will be punished" (verse 22). At that time of judgement, the moon will be confounded, and the sun confused as the Lord took His place as King of glory in Jerusalem. What is essential for us to note is the reference to the shutting up in prison of those waiting to be punished. These verses lead us to believe that the spirit of the unbeliever is shut up on some form of imprisonment, awaiting the judgement day.

At death, the body decays in the ground. The soul is cast into darkness and no longer has any memory or consciousness. The spirit, however, appears to remain conscious and either goes to the Lord or is held in bondage awaiting the day of resurrection and judgement.

Chapter 9 -
The Resurrection and the Judgement

The Bible teaches that after death, we will stand before our Creator to be judged.

[27] And just as it is appointed for man to die once, and after that comes judgment, [28] so Christ, having been offered once to bear the sins of many, will appear a second time, not to deal with sin but to save those who are eagerly waiting for him. (Hebrews 9)

For that judgement to take place, the dead must first be raised to life.

RESURRECTION

The Old Testament saints accepted the resurrection of the dead as a fact. Listen to the words of Job:

[25] For I know that my Redeemer lives, and at the last he will stand upon the earth. [26] And after my skin has been thus destroyed, yet in my flesh I shall see God, [27] whom I shall see for myself, and my eyes shall behold, and not another. My heart faints within me! (Job 19)

While His skin would be destroyed, Job had confidence that he would see God in his flesh. He had an understanding that he would receive a new body of flesh and see God after he died.

The Resurrection and the Judgement

Not every Jew believed in the resurrection of the dead. The Sadducees of the New Testament did not accept this truth (Matthew 22:23). On one occasion, they came to Jesus to challenge this belief. Listen to the words of Jesus to these unbelieving Sadducees:

[29] But Jesus answered them, "You are wrong, because you know neither the Scriptures nor the power of God. [30] For in the resurrection they neither marry nor are given in marriage, but are like angels in heaven. [31] And as for the resurrection of the dead, have you not read what was said to you by God: [32] 'I am the God of Abraham, and the God of Isaac, and the God of Jacob'? He is not God of the dead, but of the living." [33] And when the crowd heard it, they were astonished at his teaching. (Matthew 22)

To those who refused to believe in the resurrection, Jesus said: "You are wrong because you know neither the Scriptures nor the power of God" (verse 29). There can be no doubt that Jesus believed that the Scriptures taught the resurrection of the dead.

Speaking to Martha after the death of her brother Lazarus, Jesus said: "Your brother will rise again" (John 11:23). Listen to the response of Martha to this statement from her Lord:

[24] Martha said to him, "I know that he will rise again in the resurrection on the last day." (John 11)

Martha believed in the resurrection of the dead on the last day. Jesus would go on that day to demonstrate the power of the resurrection by raising Lazarus from the dead.

Annihilation and Eternal Punishment

In Luke 14, Jesus told those who were listening to Him that when they prepared a banquet, they were to invite those who could not pay them back—the poor and the needy. He went on to tell them they would receive their reward at the resurrection:

[14] and you will be blessed, because they cannot repay you. For you will be repaid at the resurrection of the just." (Luke 14)

Listen to the Lord's instruction in John 5:

[28] Do not marvel at this, for an hour is coming when all who are in the tombs will hear his voice [29] and come out, those who have done good to the resurrection of life, and those who have done evil to the resurrection of judgment. (John 5)

According to Jesus, there was a day coming when those who were in the graves would hear His voice. They would be given life again. Some would experience the resurrection of life, and others would experience a resurrection of judgement. In other words, there would be a resurrection of both the believer and the unbeliever.

In his defence before Governor Felix, the apostle Paul had this to say:

[14] But this I confess to you, that according to the Way, which they call a sect, I worship the God of our fathers, believing everything laid down by the Law and written in the Prophets, [15] having a hope in God, which these men themselves accept, that there will be a resurrection of both the just and the unjust. (Acts 24)

The Resurrection and the Judgement

Paul told Felix that he preached what was taught in the Law and the Prophets that there would be a resurrection of both the just and the unjust. The resurrection was not only for the believer but for the unbeliever as well.

The apostle suffered because they preached about the resurrection of the dead. We have an example of this in Acts 4:

[4:1] And as they were speaking to the people, the priests and the captain of the temple and the Sadducees came upon them, [2] greatly annoyed because they were teaching the people and proclaiming in Jesus the resurrection from the dead. [3] And they arrested them and put them in custody until the next day, for it was already evening. (Acts 4)

Writing to the Corinthians, the apostle Paul dealt with those who rejected the resurrection:

[12] Now if Christ is proclaimed as raised from the dead, how can some of you say that there is no resurrection of the dead? [13] But if there is no resurrection of the dead, then not even Christ has been raised. [14] And if Christ has not been raised, then our preaching is in vain and your faith is in vain. [15] We are even found to be misrepresenting God, because we testified about God that he raised Christ, whom he did not raise if it is true that the dead are not raised. [16] For if the dead are not raised, not even Christ has been raised. [17] And if Christ has not been raised, your faith is futile and you are still in your sins. [18] Then those also who have fallen asleep in Christ have perished. [19] If in Christ we have hope in this life only, we are of all people most to be pitied. (1 Corinthians 15)

Annihilation and Eternal Punishment

For the apostle Paul, the resurrection of the body was an essential doctrine of the Christian faith. To deny the resurrection was to deny that Jesus had risen from the dead. If Jesus did not rise from the dead, then our faith is vain.

There were many questions in the mind of the early believers about the resurrection of the body. Writing to the Corinthians, Paul take the time to deal with some of these questions:

[35] But someone will ask, "How are the dead raised? With what kind of body do they come?" [36] You foolish person! What you sow does not come to life unless it dies. [37] And what you sow is not the body that is to be, but a bare kernel, perhaps of wheat or of some other grain. [38] But God gives it a body as he has chosen, and to each kind of seed its own body. [39] For not all flesh is the same, but there is one kind for humans, another for animals, another for birds, and another for fish. [40] There are heavenly bodies and earthly bodies, but the glory of the heavenly is of one kind, and the glory of the earthly is of another. [41] There is one glory of the sun, and another glory of the moon, and another glory of the stars; for star differs from star in glory. [42] So is it with the resurrection of the dead. What is sown is perishable; what is raised is imperishable. [43] It is sown in dishonor; it is raised in glory. It is sown in weakness; it is raised in power. [44] It is sown a natural body; it is raised a spiritual body. If there is a natural body, there is also a spiritual body. (1 Corinthians 15)

To answer the question of what the resurrected body would be like, and to settle the doubts of those who questioned this doctrine, the apostle gives an illustration of a seed. The seed is planted in the ground and dies. Out of that death, life is born, and a new plant begins to immerge. That plant looks different from the seed. Paul told the Corinthians that they placed a perishable body in the ground, but it would be raised as an imperishable body. An earthly body was buried but rose as a spiritual body. In other words, the body we will be given will be completely different from what we have now. According to Paul, these new bodies will be imperishable, glorious, powerful and spiritual (1 Corinthians 15:42-44).

There can be no doubt that the Bible teaches that there will be a resurrection of the dead. This body will decompose in the grave, but God will raise it again, and we will stand before Him to give an account of our lives.

JUDGEMENT

The Bible teaches not only that there will be a resurrection of the body but that we will be raised to stand before God as our judge. Consider the words of the Lord Jesus in John 5:

[26] For as the Father has life in himself, so he has granted the Son also to have life in himself. [27] And he has given him authority to execute judgment, because he is the Son of Man. [28] Do not marvel at this, for an hour is coming when all who are in the tombs will hear his voice [29] and come out, those who have done good to the resurrection of life, and those who have done evil to the resurrection of judgment. (John 5)

Jesus taught that there would be a resurrection of life and a resurrection of judgement. Both the believer and the unbeliever would be raised and face judgement. Those who had done good would be raised to receive life. Those who had done evil would be raised to receive judgement.

In Matthew 25:31-4, the Lord Jesus describes this judgement.

[31] "When the Son of Man comes in his glory, and all the angels with him, then he will sit on his glorious throne. [32] Before him will be gathered all the nations, and he will separate people one from another as a shepherd separates the sheep from the goats. [33] And he will place the sheep on his right, but the goats on the left. (Matthew 25)

The resurrection, according to Jesus, will take place when He returns with his angels to this earth. On that day, all nations would be gathered to Him, and he will separate the sheep (His children) from the goats (the unbeliever). Notice that the sheep are placed on His right (the side of blessing and honour). To the goats on His left that Lord Jesus will declare:

[41] "Then he will say to those on his left, 'Depart from me, you cursed, into the eternal fire prepared for the devil and his angels. (Matthew 25)

Those who did not believe would be cursed and sent to the eternal fire prepared for the devil and his angels. Jesus ends His instruction on the judgement of those days but saying:

[46] And these will go away into eternal punishment, but the righteous into eternal life." (Matthew 25)

Eternal fire and eternal punishment will be declared for the unbeliever. Eternal life will be the inheritance of the righteous.

The Resurrection and the Judgement

Preaching in Greece, the apostle Paul told those who had gathered to hear him speak that God had "fixed a day on which He will judge the world" (Acts 17:31):

[30] The times of ignorance God overlooked, but now he commands all people everywhere to repent, [31] because he has fixed a day on which he will judge the world in righteousness by a man whom he has appointed; and of this he has given assurance to all by raising him from the dead."

Paul taught that this judgement was for both the believer and the unbeliever:

[9] So whether we are at home or away, we make it our aim to please him. [10] For we must all appear before the judgment seat of Christ, so that each one may receive what is due for what he has done in the body, whether good or evil. (2 Corinthians 5)

Both believers and unbelievers alike will stand before their judge. We will receive what is due for what we have done in the body. The challenge for us as believers, according to Paul, is to make it "our aim to please Him" (verse 9). We will all have to give an account of our lives and actions here below. As you consider standing before Him on that day, what do you suppose He will say to you? Will He be pleased with your efforts for the sake of His name?

Writing to Timothy, the apostle Paul said:

[4:1] I charge you in the presence of God and of Christ Jesus, who is to judge the living and the dead, and by his appearing and his kingdom: [2] preach the word; be ready in season and out of

season; reprove, rebuke, and exhort, with complete patience and teaching. (2 Timothy)

Paul wanted Timothy to live and minister as one who would one day be judged by God. He encouraged him, therefore, to preach the word and be ready at all times for the Lord's appearance. As a pastor, Timothy was also to reprove, rebuke, and exhort those the Lord had put under his care so that they too would be ready to stand before God on the day of judgement.

Jude told his readers that Enoch proclaimed the judgement of God:

[14] It was also about these that Enoch, the seventh from Adam, prophesied, saying, "Behold, the Lord comes with ten thousands of his holy ones, [15] to execute judgment on all and to convict all the ungodly of all their deeds of ungodliness that they have committed in such an ungodly way, and of all the harsh things that ungodly sinners have spoken against him." (Jude)

According to Jude, the Lord God will come with His angels to execute this judgement.

Paul warned those who refused to repent of their sin that they were storing up wrath for the day of judgement:

[5] But because of your hard and impenitent heart you are storing up wrath for yourself on the day of wrath when God's righteous judgment will be revealed. [6] He will render to each one according to his works: [7] to those who by patience in well-doing seek for glory and honor and immortality, he will give eternal life; [8] but for those who are self-seeking and do not obey the truth,

81

but obey unrighteousness, there will be wrath and fury. (Romans 2)

The apostle John tells us what he saw in his vision in Revelation 20. Speaking about what God revealed to him about the judgement to come, he said:

[11] Then I saw a great white throne and him who was seated on it. From his presence earth and sky fled away, and no place was found for them. [12] And I saw the dead, great and small, standing before the throne, and books were opened. Then another book was opened, which is the book of life. And the dead were judged by what was written in the books, according to what they had done. [13] And the sea gave up the dead who were in it, Death and Hades gave up the dead who were in them, and they were judged, each one of them, according to what they had done. [14] Then Death and Hades were thrown into the lake of fire. This is the second death, the lake of fire. [15] And if anyone's name was not found written in the book of life, he was thrown into the lake of fire. (Revelation 20)

In this vision, the Lord God was seated on His judgement throne. Those who were alive at the time and those who had died were all brought before Him. John describes to sets of books in his vision. First, there were what he refers to simply as "books." These books appear to contain the story of those who stood before the throne. According to Revelation 20:12, those who stood before God on that judgement day were judged according to what was written in those books. It would appear that both believers and unbelievers were judged based on what was in those books.

John, however, described a second book. This book he called the "book of life." When everyone was judged according to what was written in the first books, the second book was opened. Revelation 20:15 tells us that "if anyone's name was not found written in the book of life, he was thrown into the lake of fire." All were judged according to their deeds, but only those whose names were written in the book of life were spared the lake of fire. The book of life contained the names of those who had accepted the Lord Jesus and the forgiveness He offered. Though they too were guilty, they were forgiven by His blood and their penalty covered by His work at Calvary.

The Bible speaks plainly about the resurrection and the judgement to come. What we need to understand here is that the grave is not the end. Whether we understand this or not, the physical death of our body and soul is insufficient punishment for sin. God requires that those bodies and souls be raised from the dead to face an even greater judgement.

Chapter 10 -
The Nature of God's
Judgement

There are some truths we never like to hear. The death of a loved one, for example, is one of those truths. Truth, however, is not concerned about our feelings. Sometimes it is unapologetically brutal and harsh. This is the case with the subject we must examine in this chapter.

We have seen that the Bible teaches that after death, there will be a resurrection of both the believer and the unbeliever. After that resurrection, we will all stand before our creator to hear His judgement. The death sentence is one of the worst punishments we can inflict on a criminal on this earth. This, however, is not adequate punishment for sin, according to Scripture. Those who have died will be raised again to face an even greater penalty.

Listen to the words of Jesus in Mark 9:

[43] And if your hand causes you to sin, cut it off. It is better for you to enter life crippled than with two hands to go to hell, to the unquenchable fire. [45] And if your foot causes you to sin, cut it off. It is better for you to enter life lame than with two feet to be thrown into hell. [47] And if your eye causes you to sin, tear it out. It is better for you to enter the kingdom of God with one eye than

with two eyes to be thrown into hell, [48] 'where their worm does not die and the fire is not quenched.' (Mark 9)

Jesus told His listeners that if their hand, foot or eye caused them to sin, it would be better for them to cut it off and go through life without it than to go to hell. What is Jesus telling us here? One of the most horrible things we could ever do to our body is to cut off our limbs or gouge out our eyes. Not only is the thought of this horrific to contemplate, but the reality of living without these limbs is also difficult to accept. Jesus tells us in these verses, however, that the worst thing we could do to our body is nothing compared to the suffering and horror of hell.

Throughout history, humanity has done terrible things to one another. In the Bible, we read about those who plucked out the eyes of their captives (Judges 16:21), stoned them to death (1 Kings 21:13-14), beheaded them (1 Samuel 31:9) or burned them alive (Joshua 7:25). History recounts many other horrible deeds. Our daily news tells us of abuse, rape, murder, and many other terrible atrocities. According to Jesus, these things are but a shadow of the suffering to come for those who do not know or accept Him.

The Lord Jesus told a parable in Luke 16 about a rich man and Lazarus.

[22] The poor man died and was carried by the angels to Abraham's side. The rich man also died and was buried, [23] and in Hades, being in torment, he lifted up his eyes and saw Abraham far off and Lazarus at his side. [24] And he called out, 'Father Abraham, have mercy on me, and send Lazarus to dip the end of his finger in water and cool my tongue, for I am in anguish in this flame.' (Luke 16)

Both of these men died. Lazarus, the poor man, was carried by the angels to Abraham's side. The rich man, however, went to Hades. Notice what Jesus tells us about the rich man in Hades. He was in torment. He was very conscious of this torment and longed for relief but could find none. He begged to have Lazarus, his servant, dip his finger in some water and place it on his tongue to cool it. This might appear to be a small thing, but in the suffering, the rich man was enduring, even this small gesture would have provided a measure of relief. Notice also in verse 24 that the rich man described himself as being in anguish in flames. He was conscious of his suffering.

Notice also that the rich man does not ask to be released from Hades. He knew he would never be released. He begs for a small act of kindness and compassion. Abraham reminds the rich man, however, that no compassion or relief was possible because those who could offer any such hope could never cross over to help them:

[26] And besides all this, between us and you a great chasm has been fixed, in order that those who would pass from here to you may not be able, and none may cross from there to us.' (Luke 16)

Jesus describes hell in this parable as a place of torment where no compassion or hope could ever be offered. There is no expectation of relief. No mercy of God can touch the border of hell. There is a great divide between heaven and hell so that nothing of heaven can cross over, and nothing of hell can reach out to heaven.

On one occasion, Jesus travelled to the region of the Gerasenes. A man lived in that region who was possessed by demons. When

Jesus encountered the man, he commanded the unclean spirits to come out of him (Luke 8:29). Notice the response of these unclean spirits to the command of Jesus:

[31] And they begged him not to command them to depart into the abyss. [32] Now a large herd of pigs was feeding there on the hillside, and they begged him to let them enter these. So he gave them permission. [33] Then the demons came out of the man and entered the pigs, and the herd rushed down the steep bank into the lake and drowned. (Luke 8)

The evil spirits who possessed the man begged Jesus not to send them to the abyss. The abyss is generally understood to refer to the bottomless pit of hell. These demonic spirits feared being sent to this place. They understood it better than anyone else, and although they were evil and delighted in evil, they wanted to avoid hell. This story shows us that even the evil spirits of Satan detest hell and its suffering.

In Matthew 13, Jesus explains the parable of the weeds to His disciples. Listen to what he tells them:

[40] Just as the weeds are gathered and burned with fire, so will it be at the end of the age. [41] The Son of Man will send his angels, and they will gather out of his kingdom all causes of sin and all law-breakers, [42] and throw them into the fiery furnace. In that place there will be weeping and gnashing of teeth. (Matthew 13)

The weeds are those who have rejected the Lord Jesus. The Lord tells us that the day is coming when they will be gathered and thrown into a fiery furnace. Jesus describes this place as a place where there will be "weeping and gnashing of teeth" (verse 42).

Annihilation and Eternal Punishment

Later in Matthew 13, Jesus compares the judgment to a fishing net:

[47] "Again, the kingdom of heaven is like a net that was thrown into the sea and gathered fish of every kind. [48] When it was full, men drew it ashore and sat down and sorted the good into containers but threw away the bad. [49] So it will be at the end of the age. The angels will come out and separate the evil from the righteous [50] and throw them into the fiery furnace. In that place there will be weeping and gnashing of teeth. (Matthew 13)

Just as the fisherman who draws his net into the boat separates the good fish from the bad, so the day is coming when those who belong to Jesus will be separated from those who have rejected Him. Those who do not belong to Jesus will be thrown into a fiery furnace where there will be weeping and gnashing of teeth (Matthew 13:50)

Jesus told His disciples one day that people of Gentile origin would come to know him while those of His own people (Jews) would be cast into outer darkness where there would be "weeping and gnashing of teeth" (Matthew 8:12).

The phrase "weeping and gnashing of teeth" details the type of punishment that awaits those who are cast into hell. The word "weeping" in the Greek language is "klauthmós," and can be defined as weeping, wailing, lamenting, or grief. The word "gnashing" refers to the grinding of teeth together and describes a person who is either in a fit of rage or in intense pain and suffering.

The writer to the Hebrews has this to say about the judgement to come:

The Nature of God's Judgement

[26] For if we go on sinning deliberately after receiving the knowledge of the truth, there no longer remains a sacrifice for sins, [27] but a fearful expectation of judgment, and a fury of fire that will consume the adversaries. (Hebrews 10)

Those who reject the offer of salvation through Jesus Christ await a fearful judgement and a fury of fire. The Greek word for translated "fearful" in verse 27 is the word "phoberós" which can also be interpreted as "dreadful," "terrible," or "horrifying." Verse 27 not only describes the judgement as "fearful," but also as a "fury of fire." The word "fury" conveys the intensity of this fiery wrath of God.

Paul told the Thessalonians that God would grant them relieve by inflicting vengeance in flaming fire on those who do not know God and on those who do not obey the gospel of the Lord Jesus:

[5] This is evidence of the righteous judgment of God, that you may be considered worthy of the kingdom of God, for which you are also suffering— [6] since indeed God considers it just to repay with affliction those who afflict you, [7] and to grant relief to you who are afflicted as well as to us, when the Lord Jesus is revealed from heaven with his mighty angels [8] in flaming fire, inflicting vengeance on those who do not know God and on those who do not obey the gospel of our Lord Jesus. (2 Thessalonians 1)

Speaking about the destiny of Satan, the false prophet and the beast of Revelation, the apostle John tells us:

[10] and the devil who had deceived them was thrown into the lake of fire and sulfur where the beast and the false prophet were,

and they will be tormented day and night forever and ever.
(Revelation 20)

The torment the devil, the false prophet and the beast experienced was day and night. They had no relief from their suffering. No moment of peace or rest—only constant pain and agony.

While the Bible does not give us specific details about hell, we have enough to recognize that it is worse than anything we could suffer on this earth. It is a place that even demons fear to go. There in hell, there will be weeping, wailing and gnashing of teeth. All possibility of divine intervention is removed, and no mercy or compassion will be offered to those who suffer. They will be in a place described as a place of fiery darkness and suffering, the likes of which we have never seen on this earth.

Chapter 11 - The Duration of Hell's Suffering

In any earthly court of law, when a sentence is passed, the judge will issue an amount of time the criminal will need to spend in prison before his or her crime is paid in full. Sometimes that crime is so awful that the judge will issue a life sentence. This means that death alone will free the guilty party from his or her prison cell.

God will judge the world, as well. The sentence for those who do not know him is the suffering and agony of hell. The question we need to consider now is this: What is the length of time God requires for the individual to pay for his or her sin and the rejection of His Son?

THE COST OF SIN

We know that the penalty for sin is death.

> [23] For the wages of sin is death, but the free gift of God is eternal life in Christ Jesus our Lord. (Romans 6)

> [4] Behold, all souls are mine; the soul of the father as well as the soul of the son is mine: the soul who sins shall die. (Ezekiel 18)

The death of the sinner, however, did not remove sin or the effects of sin. Imagine that a loved one was murdered by a criminal and sentenced to life in prison. Will that sentence bring back your loved one? What if the judge sentenced the criminal to death? Would that change the fact that you now live the rest of your life without a partner or child? The pain and suffering you endure will go on even after the death of the guilty person. This leaves us with the question: is the physical death of a criminal sufficient payment for the sin he or she committed against us? The fact that God promises to raise the dead and bring them to judgement shows us that physical death is insufficient punishment for sin and the rejection of the Saviour.

THE JUDGEMENT OF SATAN, THE BEAST, AND THE FALSE PROPHET

In the book of Revelation, John describes a time when a beast would rise from the pit of hell and come to deceive the world. John tells us, however, that this beast would be defeated:

[8] The beast that you saw was, and is not, and is about to rise from the bottomless pit and go to destruction. And the dwellers on earth whose names have not been written in the book of life from the foundation of the world will marvel to see the beast, because it was and is not and is to come. (Revelation 17)

John would go on to describe this destruction in Revelation 20:

[10] and the devil who had deceived them was thrown into the lake of fire and sulfur where the beast and the false prophet were, and they will be tormented day and night forever and ever. (Revelation 20)

When we compare Revelation 17:8 with Revelation 20:10, we see that the beast who would "go to destruction" was thrown into the lake of fire and sulphur, where he was tormented day and night forever and ever. When we think of destruction, we think of

94

physical death. The Greek word used for destruction (ESV) or perdition (KJV) in Revelation 17:8 is the word "apóleia," which is defined by the AMG Complete Word Study Dictionary as follows:

In the NT, apóleia refers to the state after death wherein exclusion from salvation is a realized fact, wherein man, instead of becoming what he might have been, is lost and ruined. Destruction, either temporal (Ac 25:16, death; Sept.: Dt 4:26; Es 7:4; Pr 6:15; Isa 34:5), or the second death which is eternal exclusion from Christ's kingdom. (Zodhiates, Spiros (General Editor), AMG Complete Word Study Dictionary, New Testament, "684 apoleia" Cedar Rapids, Iowa: L A R I D I A N)

The destruction of the beast was eternal—he would suffer day and night forever and ever. He would be aware of that suffering throughout all eternity as he lived in separation from God and His favour.

Notice also that what was true for the beast was also true for the false prophet and the devil. Scripture tells us plainly that the beast, the devil, and the false prophet will be "tormented day and night forever and ever." It appears from Revelation 20:10 that the flames of the lake of fire and sulphur do not kill Satan, the beast, or the false prophet, but keep them in this state of anguish. You cannot torment someone who is dead and unaware of that torment. Only the living can be tormented.

THE DESTINY OF THE GOATS

In Matthew 25 describes the judgement of Christ when He separates the sheep from the goats. Listen to the words of Jesus concerning the destiny of the goats who had rejected His salvation:

[41] "Then he will say to those on his left, 'Depart from me, you cursed, into the eternal fire prepared for the devil and his angels. (Matthew 25)

The destiny of those who did not accept the Lord Jesus was to be thrown into the fire that was prepared for the devil and his angels. We have already seen this fire in Revelation 20:10. This, according to Christ in Matthew 25, is the destiny of the goats. They suffer in the fire that caused eternal torment but did not kill.

DEATH IS STRIPPED OF ITS POWER

Revelation 20:11-15 describe the judgment in the last days:

[11] Then I saw a great white throne and him who was seated on it. From his presence earth and sky fled away, and no place was found for them. [12] And I saw the dead, great and small, standing before the throne, and books were opened. Then another book was opened, which is the book of life. And the dead were judged by what was written in the books, according to what they had done. [13] And the sea gave up the dead who were in it, Death and Hades gave up the dead who were in them, and they were judged, each one of them, according to what they had done. [14] Then Death and Hades were thrown into the lake of fire. This is the second death, the lake of fire. [15] And if anyone's name was not found written in the book of life, he was thrown into the lake of fire. (Revelation 20)

John tells us that he saw the resurrected dead standing before the throne of God. The books describing the lives of those who stood before the Lord were opened, and they were judged, "according to what they had done" (verse 12). The book of life was also opened, and those whose names were not found in it were thrown into the lake of fire.

What is particularly of interest in this passage is that Death and Hades gave up their dead (verse 13). In other words, their power was broken, and they could no longer hold people in the grave. Death was conquered by the resurrection power of Christ. Notice what happens when Death and Hades surrender their dead in verse 14:

[14] Then Death and Hades were thrown into the lake of fire. This is the second death, the lake of fire. (Revelation 20)

The power of death to hold its victims was broken, and it was forced to release the dead. Then it was thrown powerless into the lake of fire. Verse 15 goes on to tell us that if anyone's name was not found in the book of life, they were also thrown into the lake of fire with this powerless Death and Hades. The question we need to ask here it this: If death is stripped of its power and cast into the lake of fire, then how can it claim any victims?

Death is the price of sin. It was the curse of God upon all of creation because of sin. That power will be broken. Death will no longer have any hold. It will no longer be able to strip its victims of life. In the lake of fire, death and the grave are powerless. The torment described in Revelation 20:10 as "day and night forever and ever" will not be shortened by death, for death will have no power to relieve this agony.

THE BLESSING OF DEATH WITHHELD

In Revelation 9, the apostle John tells us about the sounding of the fifth trumpet. When it was sounded, the bottomless pit was opened, and out of the smoke of the furnace came demonic beings that looked like locusts. Verses 4-6 tells us what will happen in those days:

[4] They were told not to harm the grass of the earth or any green plant or any tree, but only those people who do not have the seal of God on their foreheads. [5] They were allowed to torment them for five months, but not to kill them, and their torment was like the torment of a scorpion when it stings someone. [6] And in those days people will seek death and will not find it. They will long to die, but death will flee from them. (Revelation 9)

These locusts tormented those who did not belong to the Lord. Notice that they did not kill them but caused tremendous suffering. This suffering was to the point where those afflicted longed to die, but death fled from them (verse 6). There are times when death is an act of grace. Death relieves those who suffer from pain. In this case, however, death would not come for those who suffered. God would not grant them this grace. Are there times when God withholds His grace and favour? This passage tells us that He withheld death from those whose suffering was so intense they longed to die.

THE FIRE AND THE WORM

In Mark 9, Jesus describes hell as a place where the worm does not die, and the fire is not quenched:

[47] And if your eye causes you to sin, tear it out. It is better for you to enter the kingdom of God with one eye than with two eyes

to be thrown into hell, [48] 'where their worm does not die and the fire is not quenched.' (Mark 9)

The idea here is that the worm continues to feast throughout all eternity. The fire continues to consume without any sign of going out. For the worm to feast, it must have something to eat. For the fire to consume, it must have something to burn. What the verse seems to be telling us is that the judgment for sin never ends. The worm continues to eat. The fire continues to burn. If everything were annihilated in hell, then the flames would eventually go out, and the worm itself would die of starvation. The picture here is one of the ongoing life in the torment of hell.

ETERNAL VERSUS FINAL JUDGEMENT

Listen to the words of Hebrews 6:

[6:1] Therefore let us leave the elementary doctrine of Christ and go on to maturity, not laying again a foundation of repentance from dead works and of faith toward God, [2] and of instruction about washings, the laying on of hands, the resurrection of the dead, and eternal judgment. (Hebrews 6)

Notice the phrase "eternal judgment" in verse 2. The question we need to ask ourselves is this: What is eternal judgement, and how does it differ from final judgement?

The word eternal in the Greek language is "aiónios." It comes from the word "aión," meaning an age of time. This has led some to conclude that the word eternal refers to the coming age. In other words, eternal judgement is the judgement that is to come in the time after the Lord's return. The problem with this definition is that it limits the Biblical meaning of the word. It does not take into account that eternal does not just refer to a time in the future but to the removal of time entirely. In other words, eternal life is not only life in a future time but a life that is no longer affected by time. It is a life freed from the curse of death—a life that has no end.

When we speak about eternal judgement, we talk about something that is to come but also a judgment that has no end. This is pictured by the Lord when He tells us that the worm does not die, nor is the fire quenched. The judgement of sin will continue forever. Judgement can only be eternal if those who are being judged continue to live. If judgement kills the guilty, then it is not eternal but final.

Jesus adds something more to this in Matthew 25:46 when He says:

> *[46] And these will go away into eternal punishment, but the righteous into eternal life. (Matthew 25)*

When Jesus tells us in Matthew 25 that the righteous will be given eternal life, but the goats will "go away into eternal punishment," He is using the same word. Eternal life is not just living in an age to come but live without end in the presence of the Saviour. Eternal punishment is not just punishment in a time to come, but a punishment that has no end.

CONSUMING THE ADVERSARIES

In Hebrews 10, the author speaks to his readers about the dangers of persevering in sin after coming to know the truth:

Annihilation and Eternal Punishment

[26] For if we go on sinning deliberately after receiving the knowledge of the truth, there no longer remains a sacrifice for sins, [27] but a fearful expectation of judgment, and a fury of fire that will consume the adversaries. [28] Anyone who has set aside the law of Moses dies without mercy on the evidence of two or three witnesses. [29] How much worse punishment, do you think, will be deserved by the one who has trampled underfoot the Son of God, and has profaned the blood of the covenant by which he was sanctified, and has outraged the Spirit of grace? (Hebrew 10)

Notice what the writer tells his readers here. He tells them that if they continued to live in sin and reject the truth of Christ and His work, then there was no more sacrifice left for their sin. Instead, they could expect the judgement of God and the fury of a fire that will consume them as enemies of the cross.

Notice the phrase "consume the adversaries." This has led some to assume that those who go to hell will be consumed or cease to exist. The passage goes on, however, to explain this more fully. The writer tells us that under the Law of Moses, a person would physically die without mercy on the evidence of two or three witnesses for disobedience to the law. Verse 29 is crucial if we are to understand what is said here:

[29] How much worse punishment, do you think, will be deserved by the one who has trampled underfoot the Son of God, and has profaned the blood of the covenant by which he was sanctified, and has outraged the Spirit of grace? (Hebrew 10)

The writer of Hebrews tells us that if a person died without mercy when he or she broke the Law of Moses, then they could expect an even greater punishment for "trampling underfoot the Son of God," "profaning the blood of the covenant," and "outraging the Spirit of grace."

Hebrews 10:27 must be taken in its context. He speaks here about God consuming His adversaries, for trampling His Son underfoot, profaning His blood and outraging His Spirit. This is what we do when we reject His offer of salvation and continue to live in sin. The passage tells us that we should expect an even worse punishment than death for this sin. The Law of Moses demanded death, but there is a "worse punishment" reserved for those who turn from the Son of God. To be consumed in the context of Hebrews 10 is much more than dying and ceasing to exist. It is a fate worse than death.

DESTROYING BODY AND SOUL

Jesus makes an interesting comment in Matthew 10:28:

[28] And do not fear those who kill the body but cannot kill the soul. Rather fear him who can destroy both soul and body in hell. (Matthew 10)

In the context of this verse, Jesus reminds His followers that they would have to suffer for His name. They were not to fear their human enemies who could kill their bodies, but rather the Lord God, who could destroy both their soul and body in hell.

Let's take a moment to consider what the Lord Jesus is saying here. Notice first of all that Jesus uses two different words in this verse. The first word relates to what our human enemies can do. The word translated "kill" here is the Greek word "apokteínō." The

AMG Complete Word Study Dictionary, New Testament defines the word as follows:

615. ἀποκτείνω apokteínō. To kill outright, put to death (I) Particularly, to put to death in any manner. With the reflexive heautón (1438), himself, to kill oneself; pass. to be slain, meaning to die, perish. (II) Metaphorically, to kill eternally, to bring under eternal condemnation of death, to kill the soul, equivalent to causing the soul to perish in Gehenna. (III) Metaphorically, to destroy or abolish the enmity. (Spiros Zodhiates (ed), AMG Complete Word Study Dictionary New Testament, "615 apokteínō", Cedar Rapids, Iowa, LARIDIAN)

When using the word *apokteínō,* Jesus speaks about putting the body to death. Our human enemies, Jesus told His followers, can and may put you to death for your faith. We are not to fear what they can do to us, however. God cares for us and knows everything that happens to us. He is greater than the death of our physical bodies. He will raise them again, and we will stand before Him as faithful servants.

Instead of fearing what our human enemies can do to us, we are to fear that Lord God, who can destroy both body and soul in hell. Notice that Jesus does not use the word "kill" here. Instead, He uses the word destroy. The word destroy is the Greek word "apóllumi."

622. ἀπόλλυμι apóllumi or apolúō; To destroy, be destroyed, perish. (A) To destroy, cause to perish: (1) Spoken of things figuratively (1Co 1:19, meaning to bring to naught, render void the wisdom of the wise, quoted from Isa 29:14). (2) Of persons, to destroy, put to death, cause to perish. (a) Spoken of physical death. In a judicial sense to sentence to death. (b) Spoken of eternal death, i.e., future punishment, exclusion from the Messiah's kingdom. (B) To lose, be deprived of, of such things as reward (Mk 9:41); a sheep (Lk 15:4); a drachma or coin (Lk 15:8,9). To lose one's life or soul. Spoken of: (1) Things (Mt 5:29, 30; 9:17; Mk 2:22; Lk 5:37; Jn 6:27; Jas 1:11; 1Pe 1:7). In all these instances the verb must not be thought of as indicating extinction, but only change from one state of being to another. (Spiros Zodhiates (ed), AMG Complete Word Study Dictionary New Testament, "622 apóllumi", Cedar Rapids, Iowa, LARIDIAN)

The word Jesus uses to speak of what God does to the body and soul is different from what our human enemies do. "Apóllumi," to destroy, may imply physical death, but it also has the sense of our souls being rendered void, deprived of reward and lost. The word destroy does not necessarily imply extinction or complete cessation of life. The fact that Jesus uses two separate words in Matthew 10:28 may be of significance. At the very least, we need to be careful in using Matthew 10:28 as a proof text to say that God is going to kill the body and soul in hell. It is quite possible for the body and soul to be destroyed ("rendered void," "brought to naught," "deprived," "lost") but not killed.

THE SECOND DEATH

The book of Revelation speaks of a second death. The first death is our physical death. After this death, we are raised to life to face the judgement of God. The second death, according to Revelation 20, is the lake of fire into which Satan, the beast, the false prophet, death, Hades and anyone whose name is not written in the book of life is cast.

[13] And the sea gave up the dead who were in it, Death and Hades gave up the dead who were in them, and they were judged, each one of them, according to what they had done. [14] Then Death and Hades were thrown into the lake of fire. This is the second death, the lake of fire. [15] And if anyone's name was not found written in the book of life, he was thrown into the lake of fire. (Revelation 20)

What do we know about this lake of fire? We have already examined Revelation 20:10, which tells us that the devil, the beast, and the false prophet would be "day and night forever and ever" in its flames. The flames of this lake are eternal. The punishment in this lake is eternal destruction away from the presence of the Lord. The apostle Paul puts it this way:

[8] in flaming fire, inflicting vengeance on those who do not know God and on those who do not obey the gospel of our Lord Jesus. [9] They will suffer the punishment of eternal destruction, away from the presence of the Lord and from the glory of his might (2 Thessalonians 1)

Paul told the Thessalonians that those who do not know God and those who do not obey will "suffer the punishment of eternal destruction." The word "suffer" implies conscious awareness. The word "eternal" means never-ending destruction. The lake of fire then appears to be a place of eternal separation from God, where those who are cast in it are tormented (suffer) a never-ending punishment and destruction.

The Duration of Hell's Suffering

What are we to understand from these verses? It seems that Scripture teaches that those who reject the Lord Jesus will suffer eternal punishment. Death and the grave will be rendered powerless to relieve them of this punishment. Physical death is insufficient to pay for the rejection of Christ. This is why the unbelieving dead are raised again. The Lord does not raise us to life to take our life again. He raises the believer to eternal life and the unbeliever to eternal judgement.

Chapter 12 -
No Condemnation In
Christ Jesus

The subject of this study has been a difficult one. Some things in the Bible are difficult to understand. The destiny of the unsaved is not a pleasant one. It is for this reason that I want to take a moment to end with a message of hope.

Just as there are laws that govern our life on this earth, so there are spiritual laws that govern the universe. One of the most basic laws is the law of sin and death. Paul alludes to this in Romans 8:2 when he says:

> [2] For the law of the Spirit of life has set you free in Christ Jesus from the law of sin and death. (Romans 8)

Ezekiel 18:20 simply says: "The soul who sins shall die." This principle of sin and death goes back to the Garden of Eden, where the Lord told Adam and Eve:

> [16] And the LORD God commanded the man, saying, "You may surely eat of every tree of the garden, [17] but of the tree of the knowledge of good and evil you shall not eat, for in the day that you eat of it you shall surely die." (Genesis 2)

The rule of sin and death states that the person who sins against God and His purpose will be sentenced to death. As we have already discussed, the death referred to here is much more than the cessation of physical life—it is a separation from God and His life-giving blessings.

Whether we like it or not, Scripture teaches that judgement is coming. 1 Thessalonians 1:6-10 speaks about the seriousness of this coming judgement:

[6] since indeed God considers it just to repay with affliction those who afflict you, [7] and to grant relief to you who are afflicted as well as to us, when the Lord Jesus is revealed from heaven with his mighty angels [8] in flaming fire, inflicting vengeance on those who do not know God and on those who do not obey the gospel of our Lord Jesus. [9] They will suffer the punishment of eternal destruction, away from the presence of the Lord and from the glory of his might, [10] when he comes on that day to be glorified in his saints, and to be marveled at among all who have believed, because our testimony to you was believed. (2 Thessalonians 1)

There are some important details we need to see in these words of Paul to the Thessalonians.

Notice first in verse 6 that "God considers it just to repay with affliction..." We may not like this, but the reality is that God's punishment will hurt. From the perspective of justice, those who have broken the law must be punished. God will repay those who have broken His law "with affliction."

Second, notice the nature of this affliction that God considers just in verses 8 and 9. Paul describes 'flaming fire, inflicting vengeance," and "eternal destruction away from the presence of the Lord."

Finally, note those who will suffer this affliction in verse 8— "those who do not know God," and "those who do not obey the gospel of our Lord Jesus."

FREEDOM FROM CONDEMNATION IN CHRIST JESUS

There is hope, however, despite this devastating news. John 3:16 shares this tremendous hope with us when it says:

[16] "For God so loved the world, that he gave his only Son, that whoever believes in him should not perish but have eternal life. [17] For God did not send his Son into the world to condemn the world, but in order that the world might be saved through him. [18] Whoever believes in him is not condemned, but whoever does not believe is condemned already, because he has not believed in the name of the only Son of God. (John 3)

John tells us that God sent His Son into the world so that the world could be saved through Him. Those who believe in His Son do not need to perish but can know eternal life.

Belief in Jesus is the key to eternal life and forgiveness. What we need to understand, however, is that many people believe Jesus lived and walked on this earth who will never know this eternal life. Believing in Jesus means more than simply accepting that He lived on this earth.

To believe in someone has to do with trusting them and standing behind their purpose and work. You can believe that Jesus died on the cross for you, but do you trust that work alone for your salvation? You can accept the teaching of Jesus to be pure and holy, but are you willing to commit yourself body and soul to follow

Him and what He says? Will you suffer or even die for what He taught? To believe in the Son is to believe in His words and His work. It is to trust in what He says and rely fully on what He did.

For those who trust the Lord Jesus fully, John 3 tells us that they are no longer condemned. Paul communicated the same truth when he said in Romans 8:

[8:1] There is therefore now no condemnation for those who are in Christ Jesus. (Romans 8)

I live within five minutes from a ferry that crosses over to the province of Newfoundland, Canada. The shortest crossing takes about seven hours. Imagine that I went down to the water and decided that instead of taking that ferry, I would swim across. What would be the result? I would get so far and run out of energy and likely drown in the ocean. I could never swim that distance. The only way for me to get across safely is to get on the ferry. The ferry can do what I cannot do in my own effort and strength. As long as I am on that ferry, I can get to the shores of Newfoundland.

What Paul is telling us in Romans 8:1 is that if we are in Christ Jesus, we are safe. If we are trusting His work and His effort, we cannot fail to reach our destiny. The Lord Jesus alone can bring us to the Father. To try in my strength will result in absolute disaster. Only Jesus can take me to heaven. If I want to be free from judgement and condemnation, I must trust in what He has done alone. I must resist any effort of my own and surrender fully to Him and His work.

Listen to what the apostle Paul told the Ephesians:

[13] But now in Christ Jesus you who once were far off have been brought near by the blood of Christ. (Ephesians 2)

"Now in Christ Jesus," you have been "brought near by the blood of Christ." In other words, the result of trusting Jesus alone is that He will bring you near the Father. He does this by His blood spilled on the cross. The cross pays the penalty for all my sin and sets me free from its condemnation.

HOW MUCH BELIEF IS REQUIRED?

We have seen that those who believe in Christ Jesus and His work will not perish but have everlasting life (John 3:16). We have also learned that to believe in Jesus is to put our trust in Him and His work. Some people say: "I don't know if I have enough belief to be assured of my salvation." I want to touch on this before closing.

When Jesus was hanging on the cross, two criminals hung with him—one on each side. Luke 23 recounts the story of a conversation that took place between the three who hung on those crosses.

[39] One of the criminals who were hanged railed at him, saying, "Are you not the Christ? Save yourself and us!" [40] But the other rebuked him, saying, "Do you not fear God, since you are under the same sentence of condemnation? [41] And we indeed justly, for we are receiving the due reward of our deeds; but this man has done nothing wrong." [42] And he said, "Jesus, remember me when you come into your kingdom." [43] And he said to him, "Truly, I say to you, today you will be with me in paradise." (Luke 23)

No Condemnation in Christ Jesus

One of the criminals beside Jesus began to criticize the Lord, wondering why he did not save them if He was the Christ. He could not believe Jesus was the Messiah because He did not spare them from this cruel death. He rejected Jesus as the Messiah. The criminal on the other side, however, rebuked him. He reminded his partner that they deserved this sentence of death because of what they did. Jesus, on the other hand, had done nothing wrong. Turning to the Lord Jesus that day, he cried out, Jesus, remember me when you come into your kingdom." This statement is powerful. It shows us that this man believed Jesus to be the Messiah. He knew Him to be innocent of any sin. He knew Him to be the king of an eternal kingdom. He confessed his sin but came to Jesus and asked Him to remember Him when He returned to His kingdom. He did not trust his goodness. He knew that if He would ever see the kingdom of heaven, it would only be because of the grace of Jesus. He cast himself on Jesus that day and cried out for mercy.

The words of Jesus must have encouraged the penitent sinner on the cross: "Today, you will be with me in paradise" (Luke 23:43). At the very hour of death, the criminal on the cross put his confidence in the Lord Jesus and cried out to Him for salvation. Jesus heard that prayer and rescued him from condemnation. I don't know who heard the conversation that took place between Jesus and the two men crucified with Him. I believe, however, that many similar conversations take place on deathbeds all around the world.

This man had no opportunity to live out his faith in Christ. To those who knew him, he was a sinner who deserved to die. Were it not for the record we have here in Scripture about this conversation with Jesus, we would assume that he died without knowing or trusting Jesus. This is not the case. In the moments before He died, He cried out to the Saviour and experienced His marvellous grace. We do not know what takes place in those final moments before death. Destinies are changed in those last breaths.

Jesus told that story of a man who needed labourers for His vineyard. He went out early in the morning to hire some men. They agreed to work for him for a denarius. He went out later in the day to find more workers, and they too agreed to work for a denarius for the day. This was repeated several times until finally, at the eleventh hour, he brought the last workers to the vineyard to finish the job. When the day ended, the master gathered his workers together to pay them. Those who had come last were paid first. They received a denarius for the work they had done from the eleventh hour. Those who worked longer hours expected to receive more money. When they received the same amount of money as those who had come last, however, they complained to the master. The master, however, told them that everyone would receive the same salary for their work. "I choose to give to this last worker as I give to you," he said, "do you begrudge my generosity" (Matthew 20:14-15).

The lesson of this parable is this. You may have great faith and belief in the Lord Jesus and served Him for many years. This, however, does not give you any greater salvation than those who accept Him in the final hour of their life. The salvation of God is as real for the one who accepts the Lord in the last days of their life as it is for the one who has served all their life. It is as real for the one who has great faith as it is for the one whose faith has not matured.

No Condemnation in Christ Jesus

Listen to the words of the apostle Paul to the Corinthians:

[10] According to the grace of God given to me, like a skilled master builder I laid a foundation, and someone else is building upon it. Let each one take care how he builds upon it. [11] For no one can lay a foundation other than that which is laid, which is Jesus Christ. [12] Now if anyone builds on the foundation with gold, silver, precious stones, wood, hay, straw— [13] each one's work will become manifest, for the Day will disclose it, because it will be revealed by fire, and the fire will test what sort of work each one has done. [14] If the work that anyone has built on the foundation survives, he will receive a reward. [15] If anyone's work is burned up, he will suffer loss, though he himself will be saved, but only as through fire. (1 Corinthians 3)

Paul illustrates the Christian life as a building built on the foundation of Christ and His work. He encouraged believers to build on that foundation using gold, silver and precious stones so that when the work was tested by fire, it would withstand the test. Each of us will stand before the Lord God to give an account of our life. Notice, however, that some people will build on the foundation using wood, hay and straw. When the fire of God's judgement tests their work, it will be burnt up, and nothing will survive except the foundation on which they built.

Listen to what Paul has to say to those who built on the foundation of Christ with wood, hay and straw:

[15] If anyone's work is burned up, he will suffer loss, though he himself will be saved, but only as through fire. (1 Corinthians 3)

While the matter of what it means to build with wood, hay and straw is a subject for another study, what is important for us to note here is that those who build with wrong motives or in a way that is not according to God's purpose will suffer loss. We are not told what that loss is, but what is clear from the words of Paul is that despite the failure of all their efforts, the foundation is sufficient to save them. These individuals may have wasted their lives on futile efforts, but their salvation is still secure because they have been placed on the foundation of Christ and His work.

What we need to understand is this. Not all those who belong to Christ will serve Him as He requires. Some believers will waste their lives. Some believers will not tap into the resources that are available to them in Christ Jesus. Some will struggle with sin and worldly ways. They will not look much like Christians at all. What they have built in their lifetime looks very much like what the world builds using wood, hay and straw. It will all pass away. They are not laying up for themselves treasures in heaven but investing in this world and its ways.

Paul tells us that when they stand before God, they will see all of this burnt by the fire of His judgement. They will stand with nothing to offer their Lord for a life lived on this earth. They will not be banished from His presence, however, because they do belong to Him, but they will suffer loss.

What I am saying here is this: We do not know who belongs to the Lord. We cannot judge who will escape the condemnation and who will be with the Lord Jesus. Those who have lived ungodly lives may open their hearts in their dying moments and experience His grace.

Those who have not demonstrated their faith on this earth, while they suffer loss may still be children of God.

I have come to know many people I call "the abandoned children of the faith." These individuals seem to fall into two categories. First, some have been hurt by the church. These individuals may not even go to church anymore because of the deep pain they have experienced at the hands of fellow believers. Some are so hurt they have wandered from the truth and want nothing more to do with fellow believers. These individuals may still belong to the Lord God, but they have chosen to be disconnected from the fellowship of believers.

The second category of believers is often found in churches that no longer preach the gospel. These individuals have had a salvation experience, but because they are not part of a church that explains these things, they are barely aware of what happened to them. They do not have a full understanding of the truth because they are in churches that, in some cases, mock the idea of being born again. These children of God have known nothing other than the one church they have attended. There may not even be another church that preaches the gospel in their region.

Others in this same group may come from another religion other than Christianity. Reports are coming in from many Muslim countries of individuals who have had visions of Christ and come to know Him through those visions. They do not have a copy of a Bible, however, to be able to understand anything more about Him and so they are starved for the truth.

These children of God have not had the opportunity to hear the truth preached every Sunday. Some have no Bible to read or material that will help them understand what happened to them when they encountered Christ. It is all too easy for us to say that anyone who cannot theologically explain their salvation isn't a Christian. We can indeed see evidence of faith by the way a person lives, but the reality is that there are people who do not live the Christian life as Christ intended who still belong to Him. They have never been discipled or taught the way of the Lord.

While we may not always be able to distinguish the true believer, the Lord knows who belongs to Him. Nahum tells us:

[7] The LORD is good, a stronghold in the day of trouble; he knows those who take refuge in him. (Nahum 1)

None who take refuge in Jesus will perish. There is hope in the person of the Lord Jesus and His sacrifice for sin. The criminal crucified next to Jesus, in his dying hours, recognized his guilt and asked Jesus to remember him. That's all it took. None of his friends would ever know that he made that request. He may have felt unworthy of any mercy from Christ. That simple request, however, changed his destiny. He didn't have time to experience a change in his heart. All he had was the word of Christ that he would be with Him in paradise.

The grace of Christ is offered to all who will come to Him. We come unworthily into His presence to receive this pardon and gift of life. We stand before Him, having all fallen short of His standard, but He is willing to accept us if we trust in His work. Considering the subject of this study, let me challenge every reader to be sure that they turn to Jesus as the source of hope and forgiveness. It is not His will that any should perish.

[3] This is good, and it is pleasing in the sight of God our Savior, [4] who desires all people to be saved and to come to the knowledge of the truth. [5] For there is one God, and there is one mediator between God and men, the man Christ Jesus, [6] who gave himself as a ransom for all, which is the testimony given at the proper time. (1 Timothy 2)

Light To My Path Book Distribution

Light To My Path Book Distribution (LTMP) is a book writing and distribution ministry reaching out to needy Christian workers in Asia, Latin America, and Africa. Many Christian workers in developing countries do not have the resources necessary to obtain Bible training or purchase Bible study materials for their ministries and personal encouragement.

F. Wayne Mac Leod is a member of Action International Ministries and has been writing these books with a goal to distribute them freely to needy pastors and Christian workers around the world.

These books are being used in preaching, teaching, evangelism and encouragement of local believers in over sixty countries. Books have now been translated into several languages. The goal is to make them available to as many believers as possible.

The ministry of LTMP is a faith-based ministry, and we trust the Lord for the resources necessary to distribute the books for the encouragement and strengthening of believers around the world. Would you pray that the Lord would open doors for the translation and further distribution of these books? For more information about Light To My Path Book Distribution visit our website at www.lighttomypath.ca

Printed in Great Britain
by Amazon

82903626R00068

but obey unrighteousness, there will be wrath and fury. (Romans 2)

The apostle John tells us what he saw in his vision in Revelation 20. Speaking about what God revealed to him about the judgement to come, he said:

[11] Then I saw a great white throne and him who was seated on it. From his presence earth and sky fled away, and no place was found for them. [12] And I saw the dead, great and small, standing before the throne, and books were opened. Then another book was opened, which is the book of life. And the dead were judged by what was written in the books, according to what they had done. [13] And the sea gave up the dead who were in it, Death and Hades gave up the dead who were in them, and they were judged, each one of them, according to what they had done. [14] Then Death and Hades were thrown into the lake of fire. This is the second death, the lake of fire. [15] And if anyone's name was not found written in the book of life, he was thrown into the lake of fire. (Revelation 20)

In this vision, the Lord God was seated on His judgement throne. Those who were alive at the time and those who had died were all brought before Him. John describes to sets of books in his vision. First, there were what he refers to simply as "books." These books appear to contain the story of those who stood before the throne. According to Revelation 20:12, those who stood before God on that judgement day were judged according to what was written in those books. It would appear that both believers and unbelievers were judged based on what was in those books.

season; reprove, rebuke, and exhort, with complete patience and teaching. (2 Timothy)

Paul wanted Timothy to live and minister as one who would one day be judged by God. He encouraged him, therefore, to preach the word and be ready at all times for the Lord's appearance. As a pastor, Timothy was also to reprove, rebuke, and exhort those the Lord had put under his care so that they too would be ready to stand before God on the day of judgement.

Jude told his readers that Enoch proclaimed the judgement of God:

[14] It was also about these that Enoch, the seventh from Adam, prophesied, saying, "Behold, the Lord comes with ten thousands of his holy ones, [15] to execute judgment on all and to convict all the ungodly of all their deeds of ungodliness that they have committed in such an ungodly way, and of all the harsh things that ungodly sinners have spoken against him." (Jude)

According to Jude, the Lord God will come with His angels to execute this judgement.

Paul warned those who refused to repent of their sin that they were storing up wrath for the day of judgement:

[5] But because of your hard and impenitent heart you are storing up wrath for yourself on the day of wrath when God's righteous judgment will be revealed. [6] He will render to each one according to his works: [7] to those who by patience in well-doing seek for glory and honor and immortality, he will give eternal life; [8] but for those who are self-seeking and do not obey the truth,

81

The Resurrection and the Judgement

Preaching in Greece, the apostle Paul told those who had gathered to hear him speak that God had "fixed a day on which He will judge the world" (Acts 17:31):

[30] The times of ignorance God overlooked, but now he commands all people everywhere to repent, [31] because he has fixed a day on which he will judge the world in righteousness by a man whom he has appointed; and of this he has given assurance to all by raising him from the dead."

Paul taught that this judgement was for both the believer and the unbeliever:

[9] So whether we are at home or away, we make it our aim to please him. [10] For we must all appear before the judgment seat of Christ, so that each one may receive what is due for what he has done in the body, whether good or evil. (2 Corinthians 5)

Both believers and unbelievers alike will stand before their judge. We will receive what is due for what we have done in the body. The challenge for us as believers, according to Paul, is to make it "our aim to please Him" (verse 9). We will all have to give an account of our lives and actions here below. As you consider standing before Him on that day, what do you suppose He will say to you? Will He be pleased with your efforts for the sake of His name?

Writing to Timothy, the apostle Paul said:

[4:1] I charge you in the presence of God and of Christ Jesus, who is to judge the living and the dead, and by his appearing and his kingdom: [2] preach the word; be ready in season and out of

would be raised to receive life. Those who had done evil would be raised to receive judgement.

In Matthew 25:31-4, the Lord Jesus describes this judgement.

[31] "When the Son of Man comes in his glory, and all the angels with him, then he will sit on his glorious throne. [32] Before him will be gathered all the nations, and he will separate people one from another as a shepherd separates the sheep from the goats. [33] And he will place the sheep on his right, but the goats on the left. (Matthew 25)

The resurrection, according to Jesus, will take place when He returns with his angels to this earth. On that day, all nations would be gathered to Him, and he will separate the sheep (His children) from the goats (the unbeliever). Notice that the sheep are placed on His right (the side of blessing and honour). To the goats on His left that Lord Jesus will declare:

[41] "Then he will say to those on his left, 'Depart from me, you cursed, into the eternal fire prepared for the devil and his angels. (Matthew 25)

Those who did not believe would be cursed and sent to the eternal fire prepared for the devil and his angels. Jesus ends His instruction on the judgement of those days but saying:

[46] And these will go away into eternal punishment, but the righteous into eternal life." (Matthew 25)

Eternal fire and eternal punishment will be declared for the unbeliever. Eternal life will be the inheritance of the righteous.